3 tres

¡En español!

LECTURAS PARA TODOS

with TEST PREPARATION

McDougal Littell

A DIVISION OF HOUGHTON MIFFLIN COMPANY

Evanston, Illinois • Boston • Dallas

Table of Contents

Academic and Informational Readings 115

Test Preparation Strategies

Introducing *Lecturas para todos*

Lecturas para todos
is a new kind of reading text.
As you will see, this book helps
you become an active reader.
It is a book to mark up, to
write in, and to make your
own. You can use it in class
and take it home.

Reading Skills Improvement— in Spanish *and* English

You will read selections from your textbook, as well as great literature. In addition, you will learn how to understand the types of texts you read in classes, on tests, and in the real world. You will also study and practice specific strategies for taking standardized tests.

Help for Reading

Many readings in Spanish are challenging the first time you encounter them. *Lecturas para todos* helps you understand these readings. Here's how.

Para leer The page before each reading gives you background information about the reading and a key to understanding the selection.

> **Reading Strategy** Reading strategies help you decide how to approach the material.

> **What You Need to Know** A preview of every selection tells you what to expect before you begin reading.

Reading Tips Useful, specific reading tips appear at points where language is difficult.

A pensar... Point-of-use, critical-thinking questions help you analyze content as you read.

Márcalo This feature invites you to mark up the text by underlining and circling words and phrases right on the page.

Gramática As you read, this feature highlights key grammar concepts.

Vocabulario This feature helps you with the new vocabulary as you read the selection.

Análisis This feature appears in the *Literatura adicional* section and encourages you to focus on one aspect of literary analysis as you read.

Reader's Success Strategy These notes give useful and fun tips and strategies for comprehending the selection.

Challenge These activities keep you challenged, even after you have grasped the basic concepts of the reading.

Vocabulary Support

Palabras clave Important new words appear in bold. Their definitions appear in a *Palabras clave* section at the bottom of any page where they occur in the selection. You will practice these words after the selection.

Vocabulario de la lectura Vocabulary activities follow each selection and give you the opportunity to practice the *Palabras clave.* Active vocabulary words from the *etapa* appear in blue.

Comprehension and Connections

¿Comprendiste? Questions after each selection check your understanding of what you have just read.

Conexión personal These short writing activities ask you to relate the selection to your life and experiences to make what you have read more meaningful.

Links to ¡En español!

When using McDougal Littell's *¡En español!,* you will find *Lecturas para todos* to be a perfect companion. *Lecturas para todos* lets you mark up the *En voces* selections as you read, helping you understand and remember more.

Read on to learn more!

Academic and Informational Reading

Here is a special collection of real-world examples—in English—to help you read every kind of informational material, from textbooks to technical directions. Why are these sections in English? Because the strategies you learn will help you on tests, in other classes, and in the world outside of school. You will find strategies for the following:

Analyzing Text Features This section will help you read many different types of magazine articles and textbooks. You will learn how titles, subtitles, lists, graphics, many different kinds of visuals, and other special features work in magazines and textbooks. After studying this section you will be ready to read even the most complex material.

Understanding Visuals Tables, charts, graphs, maps, and diagrams all require special reading skills. As you learn the common elements of various visual texts, you will learn to read these materials with accuracy and skill.

Recognizing Text Structures Informational texts can be organized in many different ways. In this section you will study the following structures and learn about special key words that will help you identify the organizational patterns:
• Main Idea and Supporting Details
• Problem and Solution
• Sequence
• Cause and Effect
• Comparison and Contrast
• Persuasion

Reading in the Content Areas You will learn special strategies for reading social studies, science, and mathematics texts.

Reading Beyond the Classroom In this section you will encounter applications, schedules, technical directions, product information, Web pages, and other readings. Learning to analyze these texts will help you in your everyday life and on some standardized tests.

Test Preparation Strategies

In this section, you will find strategies and practice to help you succeed on many different kinds of standardized tests. After closely studying a variety of test formats through annotated examples, you will have an opportunity to practice each format on your own. Additional support will help you think through your answers. You will find strategies for the following:

Successful Test Taking This section provides many suggestions for preparing for and taking tests. The information ranges from analyzing test questions to tips for answering multiple-choice and open-ended test questions.

Reading Tests: Long Selections You will learn how to analyze the structure of a lengthy reading and prepare to answer the comprehension questions that follow it.

Reading Tests: Short Selections These selections may be a few paragraphs of text, a poem, a chart or graph, or some other item. You will practice the special range of comprehension skills required for these pieces.

Functional Reading Tests These real-world texts present special challenges. You will learn about the various test formats that use applications, product labels, technical directions, Web pages, and more.

Revising-and-Editing Tests These materials test your understanding of English grammar and usage. You may encounter capitalization and punctuation questions. Sometimes the focus is on usage questions such as verb tenses or pronoun agreement issues. You will become familiar with these formats through the guided practice in this section.

Writing Tests Writing prompts and sample student essays will help you understand how to analyze a prompt and what elements make a successful written response. Scoring rubrics and a prompt for practice will prepare you for the writing tests you will take.

En voces

Point-of-use comprehension support helps you read selections from _¡En español!_ and develop critical-thinking skills.

Reading Strategy

This feature provides reading tips and strategies that help you effectively approach the material.

What You Need to Know

This section provides a key to help you unlock the selection so that you can understand and enjoy it.

Para leer _Paula_

Reading Strategy

SPECULATE ABOUT THE AUTHOR From your reading, what do you think was the age and professional status of Isabel Allende during her career? What other activities does she reveal? Do you think it is better to read a piece of literature with or without knowledge about the author? Use the following chart to organize your ideas.

Isabel Allende		
Edad	**Actividad profesional**	**Otras actividades**
Mi opinión		

What You Need to Know

The 1960s gave rise to an important generation of Chilean journalists, writers, artists, teachers, and other intellectuals, many of whom became spokespersons for social reform. Under the dictatorship of Augusto Pinochet, who seized power in a coup in 1973, many such intellectuals, including Isabel Allende, were forced into exile.

Sobre la autora

Isabel Allende, novelista chilena, nació en Lima, Perú, en 1942. Su familia tuvo que exiliarse de Chile cuando su tío Salvador Allende, el presidente del país, fue vencido por una junta militar en 1973. Isabel Allende empezó a escribir a la edad de diecisiete años y escribió su primera novela, *La casa de los espíritus*, en 1982. También ha trabajado como periodista y en la televisión.

Introducción Allende comenzó a escribir su libro autobiográfico *Paula* mientras su hija estaba muy enferma. Es una historia que ofrece mucha información y varias anécdotas sobre la familia de Allende y sobre la historia y la política de Chile. En la selección que vas a leer, Allende le habla a su hija sobre su trabajo en Chile.

Paula

A comienzo de los años sesenta mi trabajo había progresado de las estadísticas forestales a unos **tambaleantes inicios** en el periodismo, que me condujeron por
5 casualidad a la televisión.

Fue así como terminé a cargo de un programa en el cual me tocaba hacer desde el **guión** hasta los dibujos de los créditos. El trabajo en el Canal consistía en llegar puntual, sentarme
10 ante una luz roja y hablar al vacío; nunca tomé conciencia de que al otro lado de la luz

PALABRAS CLAVE
tambaleante *shaky*   **guión** *script*
inicio *beginning*

READER'S SUCCESS STRATEGY Isabel Allende uses long sentences in this selection. It may help you to read the sentences aloud and break them into parts. Pause after commas, semicolons and other punctuation marks. For example, reading lines 6-16 aloud in this way will help you visualize Isabel's job at the TV station.

APUNTES

READING TIP Note that Isabel Allende starts by talking about herself. Then, it becomes clear that she is addressing her daughter, Paula. Watch for verbs in the second person singular that indicate Allende is talking to Paula.

APUNTES

Unidad 4, Etapa 3
Paula   41

Sobre la autora
Each literary selection begins with a short author biography that provides cultural context.

READER'S SUCCESS STRATEGY
Notes like this one provide ideas to help you read the selection successfully. For example, some notes suggest that you fill in a chart while you read. Others suggest that you mark key words or ideas in the text.

PALABRAS CLAVE
Important vocabulary words appear in bold within the reading. Definitions are given at the bottom of the page.

En voces *continued*

▥ MÁRCALO ▷ GRAMÁTICA

This feature asks you to notice how a particular grammar concept from the *etapa* is illustrated. Underlining or circling the example makes it easy for you to find and remember.

A pensar...

Point-of-use questions check your understanding and ask you to think critically about the passage.

CHALLENGE

This feature asks you to expand upon what you have learned for enrichment.

▥ MÁRCALO ▷ GRAMÁTICA
You have just reviewed the use of possessive pronouns. Find and circle all the possessive pronouns in the boxed text.

A pensar...

How did Paula react when she saw her mother in TV? Write several sentences using your own words. **(Analyze)**

CHALLENGE Based on this selection, what do you think the relationship between Isabel and Paula was like? Do you think it was a good experience for Paula to see her mother on TV? Write your opinions and circle passages that support them. **(Evaluate)**

un millón de orejas esperaban mis palabras y de
15 ojos **juzgaban** mi **peinado**, de ahí mi sorpresa[1] cuando desconocidos[2] me saludaban por la calle. La primera vez que me viste aparecer en la pantalla, Paula, tenías un año y
20 medio y el susto[3] de ver la cabeza **decapitada** de tu mamá asomando tras un vidrio, te dejó un buen rato[4] en estado **catatónico**... Me convertí en la persona más **conspicua** del barrio, los vecinos me saludaban con respeto y
25 los niños me señalaban[5] con el dedo... (Michael y yo) conseguimos un par de **becas**, partimos a Europa y llegamos a Suiza contigo de la mano, tenías casi dos años y eras una mujer en miniatura.

[1] surprise [2] strangers [3] shock, fright [4] quite a while
[5] gestured to me

PALABRAS CLAVE
juzgar *to judge* **conspicuo(a)** *conspicuous:*
el peinado *hairdo* *noticeable, important*
decapitado(a) *decapitated* **la beca** *scholarship*
catatónico(a) *catatonic*

Vocabulario de la lectura

Palabras clave

la beca *scholarship*
catatónico(a) *catatonic*
conspicuo(a) *noticeable*
decapitado(a) *decapitated*
la estadística forestal *forestry statistics*

el guión *script*
el inicio *beginning*
juzgar *to judge*
el peinado *hairdo*
tambaleante *shaky*

A. Completa el siguiente párrafo con las **palabras clave** correctas. Luego ordena las letras que queden en las casillas para descubrir la palabra secreta.

Según Isabel Allende, sus primeros pasos en el mundo del periodismo fueron

___ ___ ___ ___ ___ □ ___ ___ ___ ___ ___. Unos de sus trabajos era escribir

el ___ □ ___ ___ ___ para los programas. Cuando empezó a aparecer en

televisión, Isabel no se daba cuenta de que muchas personas se fijarían en su

□ ___ ___ ___ ___ ___ ___. Cuando su híjita vio la imagen de Isabel en la

televisión pensó que estaba ___ ___ ___ ___ ___ ___ ___ ___ □. Tiempo

después, Isabel Allende consiguió algunas ___ ___ ___ □ ___ y partió a Europa.

□ □ □ □ □

B. Haz un círculo alrededor de la palabra clave entre paréntesis que mejor complete la oración.

1. Antes de trabajar en la televisión, Isabel Allende realizaba (estadísticas forestales / guiones)

2. En sus (inicios / becas) en el mundo del periodismo, pasó por varias etapas.

3. Desde que apareció en televisión, la gente la (decapitaba / juzgaba).

4. Debido a la reacción de la gente, Isabel se había convertido en una persona (conspicua / catatónica).

5. Paula se llevó una sorpresa tan grande al ver a su mamá en la pantalla, que quedó en estado (tambaleante / catatónico).

Unidad 4, Etapa 3
Paula   43

Vocabulario de la lectura
Vocabulary practice follows each reading, reinforcing the *Palabras clave* that appear throughout the selection. Words that appear in blue are *etapa* vocabulary words in *¡En español!*

¿Comprendiste?

Comprehension questions check your understanding and provide the opportunity to practice new vocabulary words.

Conexión personal

These short writing activities help you see connections between what happens in the selection and in your own life.

¿Comprendiste?

1. ¿En qué campos trabajaba Isabel Allende?

_____

2. ¿En qué consistía su trabajo en la televisión?

_____

3. ¿Por qué se fue la escritora de Chile?

_____

4. ¿De qué se trata el libro *Paula*?

_____

Conexión personal

¿Alguna vez has estado en un estudio de televisión? ¿Cómo te parece que sea la experiencia de que millones de personas vean tu cara en la pantalla y luego te reconozcan por la calle? ¿Cómo reaccionarías? ¿Cómo crees que te verían tus familiares y amigos? Escribe lo que piensas en la libreta de al lado.

Si yo saliera por televisión...
_____
_____
_____
_____
_____
_____
_____
_____

Literatura adicional

Notes in the margins make literature from the Spanish-speaking world accessible and help you read works by famous authors such as García Lorca and Cisneros.

Para leer *Romance sonámbulo*

Reading Strategy

INDICATE SOUND DEVICES Poets use **sound devices** such as repetition, rhyme, and rhythm to create mood and to convey meaning. **Rhythm,** one of the most common poetic sound devices, is a pattern of stressed and unstressed syllables. When the poem is read aloud, the rhythm can be heard in the greater emphasis on the same syllables than on the others. Choose four lines from "Romance sonámbulo" and write them in the chart below. Indicate the rhythmical pattern that you hear by marking the stressed (´) and unstressed (˘) syllables.

Romance sonámbulo

_____

_____

_____

_____

What You Need to Know

Romances are poems of Spanish origin in which the even verses have the same rhyme and, in general, each line has eight syllables. There are also *romances* in prose, whose main themes are generally a poetic point of view of a historical event. *Romances* were very popular in the the fifteenth century, since people could sing them while playing a musical instrument, dancing, or attending an informal gathering. In 1928, García Lorca wrote *Romancero gitano,* a collection of *romances* that combine both poetry and historical events. Also, some of García Lorca's *romances,* like «Romance sonámbulo,» became very popular songs.

Literatura adicional
Romance sonámbulo   101

Reading Strategy
This feature provides reading tips and strategies that help you effectively approach the material.

What You Need to Know
This section provides a key to help you unlock the selection so that you can understand and enjoy it.

Literatura adicional continued

READING TIP
These tips help you approach the selection and understand points where the language or structure is difficult.

Sobre el autor
Each literary selection begins with a short author biography that provides cultural context.

READING TIP This poem alternates the voice of the poet with the dialogue between the characters. Pay attention to the punctuation marks so that you can realize who is talking.

APUNTES

Sobre el autor

Federico García Lorca (1898-1936) nació en Fuente Vaqueros, en la provincia de Granada, España. En 1929 viajó a Estados Unidos, donde escribió *Poeta en Nueva York.* Como dramaturgo revolucionó el mundo del teatro. Sus obras se basan principalmente en situaciones dramáticas, usando un lenguaje muy atrevido para su época. En poesía se destacó con *Romancero gitano,* una colección de poemas que hablan del amor y de la política en España. Al estallar la Guerra Civil Española, fue fusilado por el ejército del general Franco.

~~~~~~~~

Romance sonámbulo

A Gloria Giner y
A Fernando de los Ríos

Verde que te quiero verde.
Verde viento. Verdes ramas.
El barco sobre la mar
y el caballo en la montaña.
5 Con la sombra en la cintura,
ella sueña en su **baranda,**
verde carne, pelo verde,
con ojos de fría plata.
Verde que te quiero verde.
10 Bajo la luna gitana,
las cosas la están mirando
y ella no puede mirarlas.

PALABRAS CLAVE
la baranda *railing*

Verde que te quiero verde.
Grandes estrellas de escarcha[1]
15 vienen con el pez de sombra
que abre el camino del alba.
La higuera frota su viento
con la lija[2] de sus ramas,
y el monte, gato garduño[3],
20 eriza[4] sus pitas[5] agrias.
Pero ¿quién vendrá? ¿Y por dónde?...
Ella sigue en su baranda,
verde carne, pelo verde,
soñando en la mar amarga.

25   —**Compadre,** quiero cambiar
mi caballo por su casa,
mi **montura** por su espejo,
mi cuchillo por su manta.
Compadre, vengo sangrando,
30 desde los puertos de Cabra[6].
—Si yo pudiera, **mocito,**
este trato se cerraba.
Pero yo ya no soy yo,
ni mi casa es ya mi casa.
35 —Compadre, quiero morir
decentemente en mi cama.
De acero, si puede ser,
con las sábanas de holanda[7].
¿No ves la herida que tengo
40 desde el pecho a la garganta?

[1] frost   [2] sandpaper   [3] thief   [4] it stiffens
[5] green plants with spiny leaves   [6] town in Spain
[7] fine cotton fabric, originating from Holland

PALABRAS CLAVE
el compadre *intimate friend*	**el mocito** *young man*	
la montura *saddle*	**decentemente** *decently, honorably*	

READER'S
SUCCESS
STRATEGY To better understand
how many people are
involved in this poem,
highlight the words that
represent each person on
these pages.

A pensar...

Make a list of the events in this
part of the poem. Consider who
is coming, whom that person is
looking for, who meets that
person, and how they feel.
(Summarize)

READER'S SUCCESS STRATEGY

Notes like this one provide ideas to help you read the selection successfully. For example, some notes suggest that you fill in a chart while you read. Others suggest that you mark key words or ideas in the text.

A pensar...

Point-of-use questions check your comprehension and ask you to think critically about the passage.

Academic and Informational Reading

This section helps you read informational material and prepare for other classes and standardized tests.

VARIED TYPES OF READINGS

The wide variety of academic and informational selections helps you access different types of readings and develop specific techniques for those reading types.

Academic and Informational Reading

In this section you'll find strategies to help you read all kinds of informational materials. The examples here range from magazines you read for fun to textbooks to bus schedules. Applying these simple and effective techniques will help you be a successful reader of the many texts you encounter every day.

115

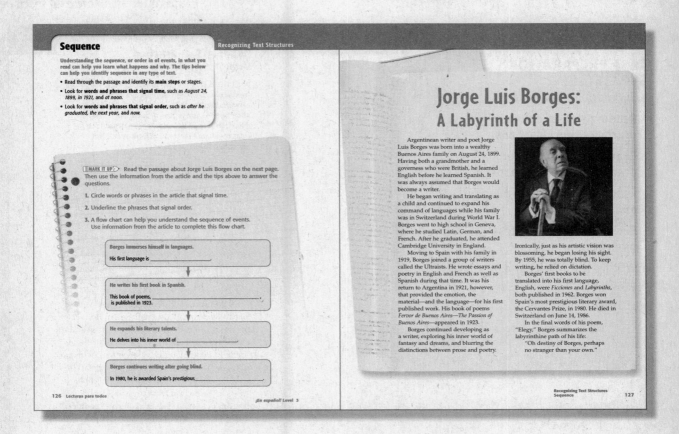

Sequence

Understanding the *sequence*, or order in of events, in what you read can help you learn what happens and why. The tips below can help you identify sequence in any type of text.

- Read through the passage and identify its **main steps** or stages.
- Look for **words and phrases that signal time**, such as *August 24, 1899*, *in 1921*, and *at noon*.
- Look for **words and phrases that signal order**, such as *after he graduated*, *the next year*, and *now*.

MARK IT UP Read the passage about Jorge Luis Borges on the next page. Then use the information from the article and the tips above to answer the questions.

1. Circle words or phrases in the article that signal time.

2. Underline the phrases that signal order.

3. A flow chart can help you understand the sequence of events. Use information from the article to complete this flow chart.

> **Borges immerses himself in languages.**
> His first language is _____

> **He writes his first book in Spanish.**
> This book of poems, _____ , is published in 1923.

> **He expands his literary talents.**
> He delves into his inner world of _____

> **Borges continues writing after going blind.**
> In 1980, he is awarded Spain's prestigious _____ ,

Jorge Luis Borges:
A Labyrinth of a Life

Argentinean writer and poet Jorge Luis Borges was born into a wealthy Buenos Aires family on August 24, 1899. Having both a grandmother and a governess who were British, he learned English before he learned Spanish. It was always assumed that Borges would become a writer.

He began writing and translating as a child and continued to expand his command of languages while his family was in Switzerland during World War I. Borges went to high school in Geneva, where he studied Latin, German, and French. After he graduated, he attended Cambridge University in England.

Moving to Spain with his family in 1919, Borges joined a group of writers called the Ultraists. He wrote essays and poetry in English and French as well as Spanish during that time. It was his return to Argentina in 1921, however, that provided the emotion, the material—and the language—for his first published work. His book of poems *Fervor de Buenos Aires—The Passion of Buenos Aires*—appeared in 1923.

Borges continued developing as a writer, exploring his inner world of fantasy and dreams, and blurring the distinctions between prose and poetry.

Ironically, just as his artistic vision was blossoming, he began losing his sight. By 1955, he was totally blind. To keep writing, he relied on dictation.

Borges' first books to be translated into his first language, English, were *Ficciones* and *Labyrinths*, both published in 1962. Borges won Spain's most prestigious literary award, the Cervantes Prize, in 1980. He died in Switzerland on June 14, 1986.

In the final words of his poem, "Elegy," Borges summarizes the labyrinthine path of his life:
"Oh destiny of Borges, perhaps no stranger than your own."

SKILL DEVELOPMENT
These activities offer graphic organizers, Mark It Up features, and other reading support to help you comprehend and think critically about the selection.

Test Preparation for All Learners

Lecturas para todos offers models, strategies, and practice to help you prepare for standardized tests.

TEST PREPARATION STRATEGIES

- Successful test taking
- Reading test model and practice–long selections
- Reading test model and practice–short selections
- Functional reading test model and practice
- Revising-and-editing test model and practice
- Writing test model and practice
- Scoring rubrics

APUNTES

Reading Test Practice
LONG SELECTIONS

DIRECTIONS Now it's time to practice what you've learned about reading test items and choosing the best answers. Read the following selection, "Ruins in the Mist." Use the side column to make notes about the important parts of this selection: important ideas, comparisons and contrasts, difficult vocabulary, interesting details, and so on.

Ruins in the Mist

High in the Andes Mountains of Peru, at an elevation of nearly 8,000 feet, shrouded in mist and clouds, lie the remarkably well–preserved and mysterious ruins of Machu Picchu. For nearly a century, archeologists and historians have studied the ruins, attempting to discover their origin and purpose. Machu Picchu, however, has not given up its secrets easily.

Adventure in the Andes The discovery of Machu Picchu in 1911 by a historian from Yale University is an adventure story worthy of the exploits of the fictional explorer Indiana Jones. Hiram Bingham taught Latin–American history at Yale, where he served on the history faculty from 1909 until 1924. In July of 1911, Bingham led an archeological team from Yale on an expedition to Peru. The goal of the expedition was to find the site of a city called Vilcabamba, known in archeological lore as the "Lost City of the Incas." Vilcabamba was a secret fortress in the Andes Mountains which the Inca had used as a stronghold during their rebellion against

¡En español! Level 3

Revising-and-Editing Test Model

DIRECTIONS Read the following paragraph carefully. Then answer the multiple-choice questions that follow. After answering the questions, read the material in the side columns to check your answer strategies.

¹The Maya was one of the importantest civilizations in Central America. ²As early as 1500 BC. the Maya lived in villages and they practiced agriculture and they used advanced agricultural techniques, such as irrigation. ³They made paper from the bark of wild fig trees and used this paper to make books filled with hieroglyphic writing. ⁴The Maya also worked gold copper and other metals. ⁵Long before the Spanish arrived, the Maya had calenders and advanced knowledge of astronomy.

1 Which of the following is the best way to revise the first half of sentence 1?

A. The Maya were one of the importantest civilizations…

B. The Maya was one of the most important civilizations…

C. The maya was one of the most important civilizations…

D. The Maya were one of the most important civilizations…

2 Which sentence in the paragraph is a run–on?

A. sentence 2

B. sentence 4

C. sentence 1

D. sentence 5

READING STRATEGIES FOR ASSESSMENT

Watch for common errors. Highlight or underline errors such as incorrect punctuation, spelling, or punctuation; fragments or run-on sentences; and missing or misplaced information.

ANSWER STRATEGIES

Verb Agreement and Comparisons *Maya* is plural and requires a plural verb form. The superlative form of the modifier *important* is not formed by adding –est.

Run–on Sentences Two or more complete thoughts run together with no punctuation is a run-on sentence.

Writing Test Model

DIRECTIONS Many tests ask you to write an essay in response to a writing prompt. A writing prompt is a brief statement that describes a writing situation. Some writing prompts ask you to explain *what, why,* or *how.* Others ask you to convince someone about something.

As you analyze the following writing prompts, read and respond to the notes in the side columns. Then look at the response to each prompt. The notes in the side columns will help you understand why each response is considered strong.

Prompt A

Because the United States is home to many cultures, it is also home to many cuisines. Think about the ethnic foods you have tasted. Which cuisine do you enjoy the most?

Now write an essay that describes your favorite cuisine. Be specific about the foods you enjoy and list the reasons why.

Strong Response

Midweek at Lincoln Prep offers a special treat. Each Wednesday, the cafeteria features the cuisine of a different culture. I've enjoyed curries from India, satays from Thailand, and falafel from Israel. Pasta from Italy is always a popular choice, as is Japanese tempura and onion soup from France. I have to confess, however, that my favorite dishes can be found south of the Rio Grande in Mexico.

I've been eating Mexican food most of my life, but it wasn't until our family spent two weeks touring Mexico last summer that I discovered how rich and varied Mexican cuisine really is. My favorite

ANALYZING THE PROMPT

Identify the topic. Read the entire prompt carefully. Underline the topic of the essay you will write.

Understand what's expected of you. The second paragraph of the prompt explains what you must do and offers suggestions on how to create a successful response.

ANSWER STRATEGIES

Draw the reader in with an interesting opening paragraph. The writer includes a number of examples to introduce her topic—Mexican food.

Include personal experiences when appropriate. The writer uses a family vacation as the backdrop for discussing Mexican food.

Para leer *Soñar en cubano*

Reading Strategy

OBSERVE HOW VERB TENSES REVEAL TIME Verb tenses show
when different events occur in time. Read Pilar's story of her
memories of the past and her plans for the future. Then select at
least five major events and place them on the time line below.
Notice the verb tense of each event. Are the events scattered on
the time line or clustered together? Can you say why?

Pasado en Cuba	Pasado en EE.UU.	Presente	Futuro

Recuerdos y planes de Pilar

What You Need to Know

Every year, many Latin American families immigrate to the United States
along with their young children. Arriving in a new country can present
special challenges for these children. Not only do they need to learn a
new language, but they have left behind a lot of memories, relatives, and
friends. As they grow up, many of them wish to go back to their native
countries to rediscover their roots, but this is not always easy. The
selection you are about to read tells the experiences of a young girl who
came to the U.S. from Cuba.

Sobre la autora

Cristina García nació en La Habana, Cuba, en 1958 y se crió en Nueva York. Asistió a Barnard College y a la Escuela de Estudios Internacionales Avanzados de Johns Hopkins University. Ha trabajado como periodista en Miami, San Francisco y Los Ángeles, donde vive actualmente con su esposo. *Soñar en cubano* es su primera novela.

Introducción *Soñar en cubano* es una novela que narra la historia de una familia cubana. Celia, la abuela, Lourdes, su hija, y Pilar, su nieta, son los tres personajes principales. Ellas hablan de los sueños y el dolor de la familia que vive en Cuba, y de Lourdes y Pilar. En esta selección habla la nieta, Pilar Puente.

Soñar en cubano

Eso es. Ya lo entiendo. Regresaré a Cuba. Estoy **harta** de todo. Saco todo mi dinero del banco, 120 dólares, el dinero que he ahorrado esclavizada en la pastelería de mi madre, y
5 compro un billete de autocar para irme a Miami. Calculo que una vez allí, podría **gestionar** mi viaje a Cuba, alquilando un bote, o consiguiendo un pescador que me lleve. Imagino la sorpresa de Abuela Celia
10 cuando me escurriera a hurtadillas por detrás de ella. Estaría sentada en su **columpio** de **mimbre** mirando al mar, y olería a[1] sal y a agua de violetas. Habría **gaviotas** y **cangrejos**

---
[1] she would smell of

PALABRAS CLAVE

harto(a)	*fed up*	**el mimbre**	*wicker*
gestionar	*to arrange*	**la gaviota**	*seagull*
el columpio	*rocking chair*	**el cangrejo**	*crab*

READING TIP This reading is mainly written in three tenses —present, preterite, and conditional. While reading the selection, pay attention to these tenses to have a clear idea of what Pilar experienced, thinks, and imagines.

APUNTES

READER'S SUCCESS STRATEGY A difficult passage is sometimes easier to understand if you put it into your own words. Try to restate what Pilar says in lines 1 to 9 in your own words. Remember to check the footnotes for help.

CHALLENGE In lines 11–16, Pilar describes the geography of Cuba. Do you think these memories are the only reason Pilar wants to go to Cuba? What is the importance of the island's geography to Pilar? Write your answer in the space below. **(Infer)**

_____

_____

_____

_____

▥ MÁRCALO ⟩ GRAMÁTICA
Read the boxed text. Then underline the verbs in the preterite and circle the verbs in the imperfect.

A pensar...

In the lines below, write two sentences from the reading that you think best represent the close relationship between Pilar and her grandmother. **(Analyze)**

_____

_____

_____

_____

_____

_____

_____

_____

_____

en la orilla del mar. **Acariciaría** mis **mejillas**
15 con sus manos frías, y cantaría silenciosamente
en mis oídos.

Cuando salí de Cuba tenía sólo dos años, pero
recuerdo todo lo que pasó desde que era una
cría, cada una de las conversaciones, palabra
20 por palabra. Estaba sentada en la falda de mi
abuela jugando con sus pendientes de perlas,
cuando mi madre le dijo que nos iríamos de la
isla. Abuela Celia le acusó de haber
traicionado la revolución. Mamá trató de
25 separarme de la abuela, pero yo me **agarré** a
ella y grité a todo pulmón. Mi abuelo vino
corriendo y dijo: «Celia, deja que la niña se
vaya. Debe estar con Lourdes.» Ésa fue la
última vez que la vi.

PALABRAS CLAVE
acariciar _to caress_   **agarrar** _to hold onto_
la mejilla _cheek_   **el (la) crío(a)** _infant_

Vocabulario de la lectura

Palabras clave

acariciar *to caress*

agarrarse *to hold onto*

el cangrejo *crab*

el columpio *rocking chair*

el (la) crío(a) *infant*

la gaviota *seagull*

gestionar *to arrange*

harto(a) *fed up*

la mejilla *cheek*

el mimbre *wicker*

A. Empareja cada **palabra clave** con la definición correcta. En la línea que figura al lado de cada palabra, escribe la letra correspondiente a la definición de dicha palabra.

_____ 1. harto   A. ave que habita cerca de las playas

_____ 2. acariciar   B. tocar suavemente con los dedos

_____ 3. gaviota   C. niño pequeño

_____ 4. gestionar   D. cansado de todo

_____ 5. crío   E. hacer arreglos para llevar algo a cabo

B. Completa los espacios en blanco con la **palabra clave** correcta. Escribe los verbos en su forma correcta. Solamente puedes usar cada palabra una vez.

Pilar quiere regresar a Cuba. Ella siempre imagina a su abuela sentada en su

_____ de _____. Todavía recuerda el día que se
     (1)   (2)

_____ fuertemente a su abuela para no irse. En estos momentos
     (3)

Pilar quisiera estar en la playa de Cuba, jugando con los _____
                                                   (4)

mientras su abuela le acaricia las _____.
                             (5)

¿Comprendiste?

1. ¿Por qué Pilar quiere regresar a Cuba?

_____

2. ¿Cómo piensa llegar?

_____

3. ¿A quién va a ver Pilar?

_____

4. ¿Cuántos años tenía Pilar cuando salió de Cuba?

_____

5. ¿Qué cosas asocia Pilar con su abuela?

_____

Conexión personal

Imagina que tuviste que salir de tu país cuando eras muy pequeño(a). ¿Qué cosas piensas que extrañarías más? ¿Tus familiares? ¿Tus amigos? ¿Tu ciudad? ¿Crees que es bueno irse a otro país cuando eres niño(a)? ¿Por qué? ¿Te parece que es una buena experiencia regresar a tu país después de mucho tiempo? Escribe tu opinión en los renglones de la derecha. Si tú viniste de otro país, cuenta tu propia experiencia.

Creo que...

_____

_____

_____

_____

_____

_____

_____

_____

_____

Para leer   *La casa en Mango Street*

Reading Strategy

CHART CONTRASTS BETWEEN DREAMS AND REALITY IN A PERSONAL NARRATIVE Maintaining a balance between dreams and reality is an important part of our growth. Do you have in your imagination a dream house or a dream room? How would you describe it? Complete the chart to compare the author's casa de sus sueños (*dreams*) and la casa en Mango Street. Consider each one from these points of view:

	La casa de sus sueños	La casa en Mango Street
Tamaño		
Habitaciones		
Patio		
Jardín		
Otros		

What You Need to Know

Moving to a new house can cause different kinds of emotions. You might feel excited about moving to a nicer, more comfortable place. If you are moving far away from your friends and places you are familiar with, it could be a traumatic experience. Or, you might become very disappointed, when the house you arrive at is not the one you dreamed of.

READING TIP This reading shows a contrast between dreams and reality. The narrator expresses the things she would like to have by using the conditional. Then, she makes comparisons by starting with the word **pero** and switching to the present tense.

A pensar...

Place a check mark next to the sentences that express Esperanza's reality. (**Compare and Contrast**)

___ **a.** No hay jardín al frente sino cuatro olmos chiquititos.

___ **b.** Tendríamos por lo menos tres baños.

___ **c.** Nuestra casa sería banca, rodeada de árboles.

___ **d.** Los ladrillos se hacen pedazos.

___ **e.** Nuestra casa tiene escaleras pero son ordinarias.

MÁRCALO ⟩ **VOCABULARIO**
Read the boxed text. Underline the things that are outside the house. Then circle the things that are inside the house.

Sobre la autora

Sandra Cisneros, la autora de *La casa en Mango Street,* nació en Chicago en 1954. Escribe ficción y poesía y vive en San Antonio, Texas.

Introducción   *La casa en Mango Street* es una novela que narra las experiencias de Esperanza Cordero, una chica que vive en un barrio latino de Chicago. Ella quiere tener una casa y escribir cuentos. En prosa sencilla y colorida, Sandra Cisneros describe los pensamientos de esta joven. Elena Poniatowska, una escritora mexicana famosa, tradujo esta selección del inglés al español.

La casa en Mango Street

Siempre decían que algún día nos mudaríamos a una casa, una casa de verdad, que fuera nuestra para siempre, de la que no tuviéramos que salir cada año, y nuestra casa
5 tendría agua corriente y tubos que sirvieran[1]. Y escaleras interiores propias como las de la tele.

Y tendríamos un sótano, y por lo menos tres baños para no tener que **avisarle** a todo el mundo cada vez que nos bañáramos. Nuestra
10 casa sería blanca, **rodeada** de árboles, un jardín enorme y el pasto creciendo sin cerca.

[1] that work

PALABRAS CLAVE
avisar   *to announce*
rodeado(a)   *surrounded*

Ésa es la casa
de la que
hablaba Papá
15 cuando tenía
un billete de
lotería y ésa es
la casa que Mamá
soñaba en los cuentos que
20 nos contaba antes de dormir.

Pero la casa de Mango Street no es de ningún
modo como ellos la contaron. Es pequeña y
roja, con escalones apretados al frente y unas
ventanitas tan chicas que parecen guardar su
25 respiración. Los ladrillos se hacen **pedazos** en
algunas partes y la puerta del frente se ha
hinchado tanto que uno tiene que empujar[2]
fuerte para entrar. No hay jardín al frente sino
cuatro **olmos** chiquititos que la ciudad plantó
30 en la **banqueta**.

Afuera, atrás hay un garaje chiquito para el
carro que no tenemos todavía, y un patiecito
que **luce** todavía más chiquito entre los
edificios de los lados. Nuestra casa tiene
35 escaleras pero son ordinarias, de pasillo, y
tiene solamente un baño. Todos compartimos
recámaras, Mamá y Papá, Carlos y Kiki, yo
y Nenny.

---

[2] to push

PALABRAS CLAVE
  soñar *to dream*
  el pedazo *piece*
  hincharse *to become swollen*
  el olmo *elm*
  la banqueta *sidewalk*
  lucir *to look, to appear*

Vocabulario de la lectura

Palabras clave

avisar *to announce*
hincharse *to become swollen*
lucir *to look, to appear*

el olmo *elm*
la banqueta *sidewalk*
el pedazo *piece*

rodeado(a) *surrounded*
soñar *to dream*
el sótano *basement*

A. Completa las siguientes oraciones con las **palabras clave** apropiadas.
Escribe los verbos en su forma correcta. Luego, ordena las letras que queden
en las casillas para completar la oración de abajo.

1. Pilar ___ ___ ☐ ___ ___ ___ con mudarse a un lugar más cómodo y bonito.

2. Ella quería vivir en un casa ___ ___ ___ ☐ ___ ___ ___ de árboles.

3. Finalmente se mudó a una casa donde los ladrillos se

   hacían ___ ___ ___ ___ ___ ___ ☐ .

4. El patiecito de la casa nueva no ___ ☐ ___ ___ ___ como Pilar esperaba.

5. Frente a la casa no había muchos árboles; sólo unos ☐ ___ ___ ___ ___ chiquitos.

Segun Pilar, la casa en Mango Street no era la casa de sus ___ ___ ___ ___ ___ s.

B. Haz una línea debajo de la opción que complete correctamente la oración.

1. Cuando la gente sale a pasear, camina por la ...

   a. casa   b. calle   c. banqueta

2. La parte más baja de una casa es ...

   a. el sótano   b. el techo   c. el olmo

3. Decire a alguien que algo va a pasar es ...

   a. soñar   b. rodear   c. avisar

4. Imaginarse lo que uno desea es ...

   a. soñar   b. salir   c. mudarse

5. Generalmente, cuando la madera se moja, también se ...

   a. sueña   b. hincha   c. luce

¿Comprendiste?

1. ¿Cómo es la casa que imaginaba Esperanza?

_____

_____

2. ¿Cómo es la casa de Mango Street?

_____

_____

_____

_____

3. ¿Dónde vivía Esperanza antes de mudarse a Mango Street?

_____

4. ¿Quiénes son los miembros de la familia Cordero?

_____

Conexión personal

¿Te has mudado de casa alguna vez? ¿Te gusta la casa donde vives o preferirías mudarte? ¿Te gustaría que todo fuera diferente o quisieras conservar algunas cosas? Completa el siguiente diagrama de Venn con cosas que no te gustan de tu casa y con cosas que te gustaría tener en la casa de tus sueños. En el medio pon las cosas de tu casa que te gustaría conservar.

Cosas que no me gustan   **Cosas que me gustarían**

Para leer   *Rigoberta Menchú*

Reading Strategy

COMPREHEND COMPLEX SENTENCES Rigoberta Menchú is an admirable international figure. When she writes or speaks, she usually combines several ideas in one paragraph. For example, here are the meaningful units inside one of her sentences:

Tenemos el reto / de construir y consolidar la democracia y la paz, / resolviendo los problemas internos y privilegiando el diálogo.

Focus first on the small units of meaning rather than on the entire sentence. Read the sections aloud. What words connect the units of meaning? Try this technique with other sentences so that you can understand them more easily. Choose another sentence from the text in bold, write it down on the lines below, and use slashes to divide it into units.

_____

_____

_____

_____

_____

What You Need to Know

For centuries, indigenous people from many parts of the world have suffered discrimination. In Guatemala, Rigoberta Menchú has dedicated her life to fighting for equality, especially the rights of native peoples. She belongs to the *quiché*, a native group of Central America that earns its living by farming and weaving. In the sixteenth century, the *quiché* wrote the *Popol-Vuh* — the main source of information about the Mayan civilization.

Rigoberta Menchú

Rigoberta Menchú cuenta una historia tan
extraordinaria como su vida. Ella se escapó de
la **represión** del gobierno de Guatemala
durante las décadas de los 70 y los 80, cuando
5 muchas personas murieron, incluyendo
miembros de la familia de Rigoberta.

Una de las razones de la represión fue la
discriminación de la clase alta y la clase
media contra los indios, quienes viven en
10 las montañas, lejos de la ciudad, y con muy
pocos recursos.

Rigoberta Menchú decidió organizar a los
indios para que se defendieran contra la
violencia del gobierno, pero luego tuvo que
15 irse de su país. Fue a París, donde Elizabeth
Burgos, una activista de nacionalidad francesa
y venezolana, la ayudó a escribir su historia.

PALABRAS CLAVE
la represión *repression*   **la violencia** *violence*

READING TIP Quotation
marks are used to indicate text
that is an exact reproduction of
a speech or writing of a person
other than the author of the
article you are reading. Look at
the selection and find the
quoted text.

APUNTES

MÁRCALO VOCABULARIO
Read the boxed text. Circle
three words that represent
social problems.

A pensar...

In the word bank below, circle
the words that indicate things
Rigoberta Menchú is concerned
about. **(Evaluate)**

murieron   París
premio   unión
entrevistas   clase alta
indios   violencia

READER'S SUCCESS STRATEGY As you read, look for main events in the life of Rigoberta Menchú. You can use a ruler to help you read slowly and deliberately. Place the ruler under the first line of text on a page. When you finish the line, move the ruler to the next line.

APUNTES

_____

_____

_____

_____

_____

_____

CHALLENGE Read the quoted text. How do you explain that the most precious treasure for Rigoberta is her ability to dream? Do you think that **interculturalidad** is the secret to achieving harmony among different peoples? Why? (Infer)

_____

_____

_____

_____

_____

_____

Por los esfuerzos para mejorar las condiciones de su pueblo, Rigoberta Menchú ganó el

20 **Premio Nóbel** de la Paz en 1992. Ella habla frecuentemente sobre la paz.

❝ **El tesoro más grande que tengo en la vida es la capacidad de soñar. En las situaciones más duras y complejas, he sido capaz de soñar**

25 **con un futuro más hermoso.** ❞

En su testimonio personal, _Me llamo Rigoberta Menchú y así me nació la conciencia_, Rigoberta Menchú cuenta cómo fue una de las víctimas del prejuicio de pertenecer a un pueblo

30 indígena, donde casi todos hablan su propia lengua, el **quiché**. Además, en sus entrevistas siempre hace referencia a la unión de los pueblos.

❝ **La utopía de la interculturalidad**

35 **debe convertirse en el motor que guíe las relaciones entre pueblos y culturas.** ❞

PALABRAS CLAVE
el premio Nóbel _Nobel Prize_
complejo(a) _complex_
el quiché _indigenous language from Guatemala_
la interculturalidad _interaction between cultures_

Vocabulario de la lectura

Palabras clave

complejo(a) *complex*

la discriminación *discrimination*

la interculturalidad *interaction between cultures*

el prejuicio *prejudice*

el premio Nóbel *Nobel Prize*

el quiché *indigenous language from Guatemala*

la represión *repression*

la violencia *violence*

A. En la línea que aparece al lado de cada par de palabras o expresiones, escribe si éstas son **sinónimos** o **antónimos**. Recuerda que los sinónimos son palabras que tienen el mismo significado mientras que los antónimos tienen significados opuestos.

1. represión - libertad _____

2. complejo - simple _____

3. violencia - paz _____

4. discriminación - separación _____

5. interculturalidad - intercambio _____

B. Haz un círculo alrededor de la **palabra clave** que mejor complete la oración.

1. Rigoberta Menchú recibió el (quiché / premio Nóbel).

2. Siempre estuvo en contra de la (interculturalidad / violencia).

3. Según Rigoberta, la (discriminación / interculturalidad) es el secreto de la unión de los pueblos.

4. Rigoberta Menchú habla (quiché / complejo).

5. En 1992, Rigoberta ganó el premio Nóbel por defender el(la) (prejuicio / paz).

¿Comprendiste?

1. ¿Cuál es el sueño más grande de Rigoberta Menchú?

_____

2. ¿De qué habla en su libro?

_____

3. ¿De qué habla en sus entrevistas?

_____

Conexión personal

Imagina que trabajas junto con Rigoberta Menchú para ayudar a los indígenas de Guatemala. ¿Qué le sugerirías? En la tabla de al lado escribe una lista de soluciones a algunos de los problemas que leíste en la selección. En la otra parte de la tabla incluye con qué otros beneficios ayudarías a los indígenas.

Soluciones	Beneficios

Para leer   *Baby H.P.*

Reading Strategy

RECOGNIZE USES OF SATIRE, PARODY, AND IRONY What advertisements, TV shows, or movies do you see that use humor about someone or something? Their humor is often based on these three devices:

Satire: use of sarcasm to make fun of someone or something

Parody: a satirical imitation of a serious piece of writing

Irony: use of language whose meaning is the opposite of
    what is intended

In the concept ladder below give examples of satire, parody, or irony in "Baby H.P."

Sátira:

Parodia:

Ironía:

What You Need to Know

The advertisements we see on television or in the newspapers are intended to sell us thousands of products every day. In many cases, the advertisers propose magical solutions to situations that are not so easy to change, and the products they offer seem to be too good to be true. In the selection you are about to read, Juan José Arreola applies this commercial formula to "invent" a magical product targeted at parents with young children.

Advertisements frequently use commands to convince consumers to buy the product offered. They also include verbs in the present tense to explain the functionality of the article advertised, and verbs in the future tense to show the benefits of using such a product. While reading the selection, pay attention to the tenses to better understand the intent of the author.

A pensar...

On the line next to each phrase, write whether the phrase is a reason (**causa**) to or a consequence (**efecto**) of buying a product. (**Cause and Effect**)

1. Ya tenemos a la venta...
   _____

2. De hoy en adelante, usted verá... _____

3. Es una estructura de metal muy resistente... _____

4. Puede colocarse en la espalda o en el pecho...
   _____

5. Ni siquiera perderá la paciencia.... _____

CHALLENGE What do you think the letters "H.P." mean? Try to remember any information you have read about cars or other machines. (**Infer**)

_____

_____

_____

_____

_____

_____

Sobre el autor

Juan José Arreola, cuentista mexicano, es uno de los escritores más originales y más importantes de su generación. Nació en Ciudad Guzmán, en el estado de Jalisco, en 1918. Publicó sus primeros cuentos en unas revistas de Guadalajara durante los años 40. Las piezas cortas escritas por Arreola son cuentos, fábulas, viñetas[1] o simplemente piezas cortas. Arreola se sirve del humor para satirizar ciertas características de la sociedad y del ser humano.

Introducción «Baby H.P.», escrita en 1952, es una pieza satírica que trata del mundo de la publicidad y los anuncios. El autor parodia los anuncios dirigidos a las amas de casa, describiendo un aparato que se pone al niño para conservar su energía y convertirla después en electricidad.

Baby H.P.

Señora ama de casa: convierta usted en **fuerza motriz** la vitalidad de sus niños. Ya tenemos a la venta[2] el maravilloso Baby H.P., un aparato que está llamado a revolucionar la economía hogareña.

· · · ·

El Baby H.P. es una estructura de metal muy resistente y ligera que se adapta con perfección al delicado cuerpo infantil, mediante cómodos cinturones, pulseras,

---

[1] short descriptions   [2] for sale

PALABRAS CLAVE
   la fuerza motriz   *power, moving force*

anillos y **broches**. Las ramificaciones de este esqueleto suplementario **recogen** cada uno de los movimientos del niño, haciéndolos converger en una botellita de Leyden[3] que puede colocarse en la espalda o en el pecho,
15 según necesidad.

. . . .

De hoy en adelante usted verá con otros ojos el **agobiante ajetreo** de sus hijos. Y ni siquiera perderá la paciencia ante una rabieta convulsiva, pensando en que es una **fuente**
20 generosa de energía.

Las familias numerosas pueden satisfacer todas sus demandas de electricidad, instalando un Baby H.P. en cada uno de sus **vástagos**, y hasta realizar un pequeño y
25 lucrativo negocio, transmitiendo a los vecinos un poco de la energía **sobrante**.

. . . .

Los niños deben tener puesto día y noche su lucrativo H.P. Es importante que lo lleven siempre a la escuela, para que no se pierdan
30 las horas preciosas del recreo, de las que ellos vuelven con el acumulador[4] **rebosante** de energía.

[3]glass jar used as part of an electric circuit
[4]storage battery

PALABRAS CLAVE

el broche *fastener, clip*	**la fuente** *source*
recoger *to collect*	**el vástago** *offspring; fig. child*
agobiante *overwhelming*	**sobrante** *leftover, surplus*
el ajetreo *bustle*	**rebosante** *overflowing*

A pensar...

Do you think that the Baby H.P. is a complex or a simple apparatus? Answer the question and list the main components of the Baby H.P. in the space below. **(Evaluate)**

_____

_____

_____

_____

_____

_____

MÁRCALO ⟩ GRAMÁTICA
Read the boxed text. Then circle the verbs in the subjunctive.

APUNTES

_____

_____

_____

_____

_____

Vocabulario de la lectura

Palabras clave

agobiante   *overwhelming*
el ajetreo   *bustle*
el broche   *fastener, clip*
la fuente   *source*
la fuerza motriz   *power, moving force*

rebosante   *overflowing*
recoger   *to collect*
sobrante   *leftover, surplus*
el vástago   *offspring; fig. child*

A. Completa el crucigrama con las **palabras clave** correctas.

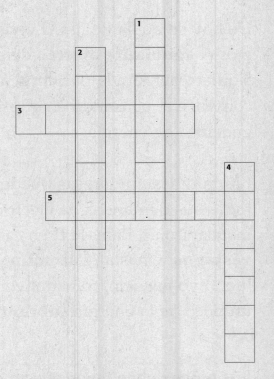

Horizontales

3. Los niños pueden ser una verdadera ... de energía.

5. Con el Baby H.P. se pueden ... los movimientos del niño y convertirlos en energía.

Verticales

1. Otra palabra para hijo es ...

2. El ... de los niños puede cansar a los padres.

4. El Baby H.P. se adapta al cuerpo del niño por medio de ...

B. Imagina que eres un vendedor de Baby H.P. y tienes que convencer a un cliente para que lo compre. Usa las **palabras clave** para completar correctamente tu discurso de venta.

¡Señora! Vea con otros ojos la _____ actividad de sus hijos. Aquí tiene
                                          (1)

la oportunidad de comprar «Baby H.P.» Este aparato convierte la energía de sus

_____ en _____ . Toda su vitalidad quedará guardada
        (2)   (3)

en un acumulador _____ de energía. Y será tan poderoso que
                          (4)

hasta podrá regalar la energía _____ a sus vecinos. ¡Cómprelo hoy!
                                        (5)

¿Comprendiste?

1. ¿Cómo son las obras de Arreola?

_____

2. ¿Para qué sirve el aparato Baby H.P.?

_____

3. ¿Cómo es el aparato?

_____

_____

4. ¿Qué ventaja tienen las familias numerosas?

_____

_____

Conexión personal

¿Cómo eras tú de niño(a)?, ¿muy activo(a) o tranquilo(a)? ¿Recuerdas alguna vez que tus padres te hayan dicho que no hicieras tantas cosas? ¿Te parece que los niños son realmente tan activos que pueden molestar a sus padres y éstos quieran evitar «el agobiante ajetreo de sus hijos»? ¿Qué actividades de los niños pueden molestar y cansar a sus padres? En el espacio de al lado contesta estas preguntas según tu punto de vista.

Yo era...

Para leer *Ébano real*

Reading Strategy

INTERPRET METAPHORS A metaphor is an implicit comparison between two things, such as "a sea of troubles." It may also be a symbol in which one thing represents another. Ébano (*Ebony*) is defined as **un árbol cuya madera es dura y negra.** Real can mean both royal and real. Read **"Ébano real"** and listen to it read aloud. What do you think this tree represents to the poet? Complete the diagram below with passages from the poem that pertain to each concept.

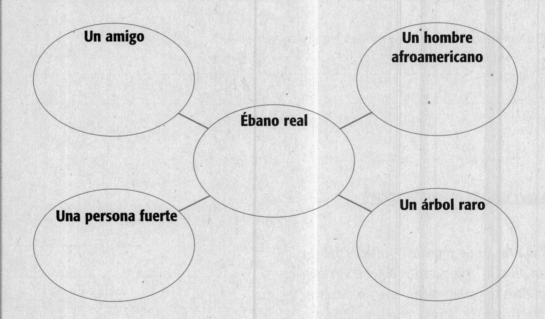

Un amigo

Un hombre afroamericano

Ébano real

Una persona fuerte

Un árbol raro

What You Need to Know

Between 1820 and 1860, thousands of Africans were brought to Cuba as slaves. Gradually, part of the African culture became part of the culture of the Americas. The poem you are about to read was written by Nicolás Guillén, a Cuban writer whose ancestry is African and European. Guillén fought for the rights of Cubans of African heritage and for the preservation of their cultural identity.

Sobre el autor

Nicolás Guillén tal vez sea el poeta cubano más conocido. Nació en Camagüey, Cuba, en 1902 y viajó a México y luego a España. En aquel entonces estaba prohibido tocar el son, un tipo de música que combina baile y cantos de estilo africano con romances castellanos de España. Guillén adoptó los ritmos[1] del son en sus poemas, creando un estilo nuevo de poesía que honra la cultura de sus compatriotas afroamericanos. Se llama «poesía negra» a la poesía de Guillén y otros poetas del Caribe. Esta poesía se basa en los ritmos y los temas folklóricos de la gente de descendencia africana.

Introducción

En el poema «Ébano real», Guillén describe un árbol viejo y majestuoso. La repetición de las frases y las palabras con sonidos africanos, como **arará** y **sabalú,** contribuyen a la musicalidad del son cubano en los versos.

[1] rhythms

READING TIP In this selection you will find two African words: **arará** and **sabalú.** From the many African groups of slaves who were brought to Cuba, the group Arará includes those who came from Dahomey, today the Republic of Benin. The name **arará** is derived from the Dahomean city of Allada. In turn, the term **sabalú** represents part of the Arará group, distinguished from the other Arará people by regional and ethnic differences. Its name comes from Savalú, a town in northern Dahomey. These two words are not common to all Spanish speakers. Listen to the audio to hear how these words should be pronounced.

APUNTES

READER'S
SUCCESS
STRATEGY Em dashes (–) are
frequently used to indicate
dialog in Spanish. Underline
the lines in the poem that
contain this mark. Note that
the dialog begins again with
the next em dash.

MÁRCALO GRAMÁTICA

There is only one verb in the
subjunctive in this poem. As
used here, the subjunctive
mood indicates that the action
of the verb has not occurred
yet. This same verb appears
more than once. Read the
poem and circle the verb each
time you see it.

APUNTES

Ébano real

Te vi al pasar, una tarde,
ébano, y te saludé;
duro entre todos los **troncos,**
duro entre todos los troncos,
5 tu corazón[1] recordé.
    Arará, cuévano,
    arará, **sabalú.**
—Ébano **real,** yo quiero un barco,
ébano real, de tu negra madera…
10 Ahora no puede ser,
espérate, amigo, espérate,
espérate a que me muera.
    Arará, cuévano,
    arará, sabalú.
15 —Ébano real , yo quiero un cofre[2],
ébano real, de tu negra madera…
Ahora no puede ser,
espérate, amigo, espérate,
espérate a que me muera.
20   Arará, cuévano,
    arará, sabalú.

[1] heart   [2] chest

PALABRAS CLAVE

el ébano ebony	**el cuévano** straw basket
el tronco trunk	**sabalú** sub-group within the Arará people
arará Afro-Cuban descendant from Dahomey	**real** real, royal

—Ébano real, yo quiero un techo[3],
ébano real, de tu negra madera…
Ahora no puede ser,
25 espérate, amigo, espérate,
espérate a que me muera.
    Arará, cuévano,
    arará, sabalú.
—Quiero una mesa cuadrada
30 y el asta[4] de mi bandera[5];
quiero mi pesado lecho[6]
quiero mi lecho pesado,
ébano, de tu madera…
Ahora no puede ser,
35 espérate, amigo, espérate,
espérate a que me muera.
    Arará, cuévano,
    arará, sabalú.
Te vi al pasar, una tarde,
40 ébano, y te saludé;
duro entre todos los troncos,
duro entre todos los troncos,
tu corazón recordé.

[3] roof   [4] flagpole   [5] flag   [6] heavy bed

CHALLENGE The poem shows dashes to indicate dialog when the man talks to the tree. Why do you think the author does not include dashes to indicate dialog when the tree responds? **(Make Judgments)**

A pensar…

1. The tree in the poem is a model of strength. Circle the words below that you think best convey this idea. **(Clarify)**

tarde	cofre
duro	real
arará	amigo
bandera	

2. Read the boxed text. Who speaks first? Who answers? What happens at the end? **(Sequence of Events)**

Vocabulario de la lectura

Palabras clave

arará *Afro-Cuban descendant from Dahomey*

el cuévano *straw basket*

el ébano *ebony*

real *real, royal*

sabalú *sub-group within the Arará people*

el tronco *trunk*

A. Empareja cada **palabra clave** con la definición correcta. En la línea que figura al lado de cada palabra, escribe la letra correspondiente a la definición de dicha palabra.

_____ 1. sabalú　　　A. canasta hecha con varillas de madera

_____ 2. cuévano　　　B. que existe de verdad

_____ 3. tronco　　　C. palabra africana

_____ 4. ébano　　　D. la parte más fuerte de un árbol

_____ 5. real　　　E. tipo de árbol y su madera

B. Completa las oraciones con las **palabras clave** correctas. Escribe los verbos en su forma correcta.

1. El hombre del poema le habla al _____ como si fuera su amigo.

2. El ébano es un árbol con madera hermosa de color negro y un _____ muy fuerte.

3. El hombre considera al ébano como una persona _____.

4. En «Ébano real», Nicolás Guillén representa su herencia africana con las

   palabras _____.

5. Nicolás Guillén compara al árbol con un objeto de carga que sufre mucho,

   usando la palabra _____.

¿Comprendiste?

1. ¿Qué relación tiene la forma musical del son con la poesía de Guillén?

_____

_____

2. ¿Contra qué protesta la poesía de Guillén?

_____

3. ¿Qué cosas le pide el autor al árbol?

_____

_____

Conexión personal

¿Piensas que una persona puede tener la necesidad de hablar con un objeto, planta o animal de la misma manera que lo plantea Nicolás Guillén? ¿Por qué crees que el autor eligió al ébano para representar a la esclavitud? ¿Qué otra cosa elegirías tú? Escribe tu punto de vista en el espacio de al lado.

Yo opino que...

_____

_____

_____

_____

_____

_____

_____

_____

_____

_____

_____

_____

Para leer   *de* Versos sencillos: *I.*

Reading Strategy

OBSERVE WHAT MAKES POETRY Poems are meant to be spoken and are often sung. Here is a poem in which the language is simple but the thought and form are complex. Four basic characteristics of a poem are rhythm, rhyme, metaphor, and inverted word order. Answer the following questions to determine if these characteristics are present in the selection.

RHYTHM Read the poem aloud. Can you tap a steady beat?

_____

RHYME Scan the sounds of the last word of each line. Is there a pattern? Give an example.

_____

METAPHOR Find a comparison between two things or a person and a thing. For example, in line 8, Martí says «**En los montes, monte soy.**» What do you think he means?

_____

INVERTED WORD ORDER To make everything work together, sometimes the poet changes natural word order. Can you find an example?

_____

What You Need to Know

The year 1868 marked the beginning of the Cuban fight for independence from Spain, which would last about 30 years. Jose Martí played an important role in the movement for independence, both as a soldier and as a poet. In addition to articles and essays directly linked to politics, he wrote many poems in which he expressed the hopes of a man who had lived many different experiences in his homeland and away from it.

Sobre el autor

José Martí, poeta, escritor y patriota cubano, nació en La Habana en 1853 cuando Cuba era todavía una colonia española. Escribió y habló a favor de la independencia de Cuba y fue exiliado a España por sus actividades revolucionarias. Luego fundó el Partido Revolucionario Cubano en 1892 y murió en una batalla por la independencia de Cuba en 1895. Martí murió como vivió, al servicio de la libertad de su patria.

Introducción La poesía de Martí es directa y sincera. Entre sus poesías más famosas se destacan los *Versos libres* e *Ismaelillo*, escritos alrededor de 1882. Aquí tienes unos versos de su libro más conocido, *Versos sencillos*, escrito en 1891.

〰〰〰〰〰〰

READING TIP Sometimes poems do not observe standard writing conventions. Often, for example, each line of a poem starts with a capital letter, even though that line is not the beginning of a new sentence. Poets are free to establish their own style. In the space below, write two lines from this poem that start with a capital letter and are *not* new sentences.

APUNTES

CHALLENGE Look at the man in the illustration on page 31. What do you think he is thinking about? Is he sad or happy? Do you believe that he is comfortable being surrounded by plants and trees? What do you think this selection is about? Write your ideas in the lines below. (Predict)

READER'S
SUCCESS
STRATEGY Note that most of
the stanzas in the poem start
with the word **Yo**. This means
that the narrator is speaking
in the first person to express
his feelings. Highlight each
line that starts with **Yo**.

APUNTES

⫼ MÁRCALO > VOCABULARIO
José Martí frequently refers to
geography, plants, animals, and
other elements of nature. Read
the boxed text and circle the
words that refer to nature or
natural phenomena.

APUNTES

de *Versos sencillos:* I.

Yo soy un hombre **sincero**
De donde crece la **palma,**
Y antes de morirme quiero
Echar [1] mis **versos** del alma.

5 Yo vengo de todas partes,
Y hacia todas partes voy:
Arte soy entre las artes,
En los montes, monte soy.

Yo sé los nombres extraños [2]
10 De las yerbas y las flores,
Y de mortales engaños [3],
Y de **sublimes** dolores [4].

Yo he visto en la noche oscura
Llover sobre mi cabeza
15 Los rayos de **lumbre** pura
De la divina belleza.

[1] to send out   [2] strange   [3] tricks, deceits   [4] pains

PALABRAS CLAVE
  sincero(a) *sincere*   **sublime** *sublime*
  la palma *palm tree*   **la lumbre** *light*
  el verso *verse*

Alas nacer vi en los hombros
De las mujeres hermosas:
Y salir de los **escombros,**
20 Volando las mariposas.

Todo es hermoso y constante,
Todo es música y razón,
Y todo, como el **diamante,**
Antes que luz es **carbón.**

PALABRAS CLAVE
el escombro *rubble, debris*
el diamante *diamond*
el carbón *coal*

1. From among the sentences below, choose the two that best represent what inspired the author to write the poem. **(Identifying Main Idea and Details)**

a. The author wishes to travel all over the world.

b. He never got married.

c. He wants to express his feelings.

d. He does not like the night or the rain.

e. He has lived through many experiences.

2. In this poem, Martí expresses a lot of optimism. Do you think he also wants to show that his past wasn't always happy? On the lines below write your opinion and some parts of the poem that support your idea. **(Draw Conclusions)**

_____
_____
_____
_____
_____
_____
_____
_____
_____
_____

Vocabulario de la lectura

el carbón *coal*	**la lumbre** *light*	**sublime** *sublime*
el diamante *diamond*	**la palma** *palm tree*	**el verso** *verse*
el escombro *rubble, debris*	**sincero(a)** *sincere*	

A. Contesta las siguientes preguntas con la **palabra clave** correcta.

1. ¿Cómo se define José Martí al principio del poema? _____

2. ¿Qué quiere entregarle a la gente? _____

3. ¿Con qué relaciona la belleza? _____

4. ¿Con qué relaciona el esfuerzo y las malas experiencias? _____

5. Los sufrimientos del poeta fueron _____.

B. Imagina que eres un poeta y estás empezando a escribir ideas para una poesía.
Escribe un párrafo con algunas cosas agradables o desagradables de la vida.
Usa por lo menos tres **palabras clave**.

_____

_____

_____

_____

_____

_____

¿Comprendiste?

1. ¿Cómo participó Martí en la lucha por la independencia de Cuba?

_____

2. ¿Qué tipo de imágenes usa Martí? ¿Qué piensas de ellas?

_____

_____

3. ¿En qué líneas del poema habla Martí de su origen?

_____

Conexión personal

Según Martí, cuanto más experiencias se tiene más se aprende. Además dice que todas las cosas buenas requieren esfuerzo. Completa una parte del siguiente diagrama con cosas nuevas que hayas aprendido en algún viaje o en alguna experiencia particular. Completa la otra parte del diagrama con cosas que hayas logrado pero que te han costado esfuerzo o problemas.

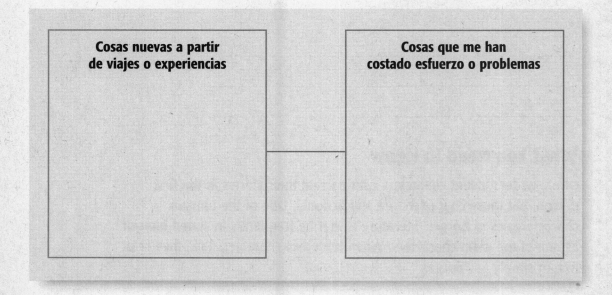

Cosas nuevas a partir de viajes o experiencias	Cosas que me han costado esfuerzo o problemas

Para leer *Jorge Luis Borges*

Reading Strategy

ANALYZE THE ROLE OF IDENTITY AND FANTASY Movies and
television often tell stories about people who are uncertain about
their identity. Think about a T.V. story or movie where you have seen
this theme. What elements does the character see as fact? Which ones
does she or he see as fiction? After the reading, complete the diagram
with elements from Borges' life that he uses in his works. Why do you
think he chose those? Would you choose the same? Explain.

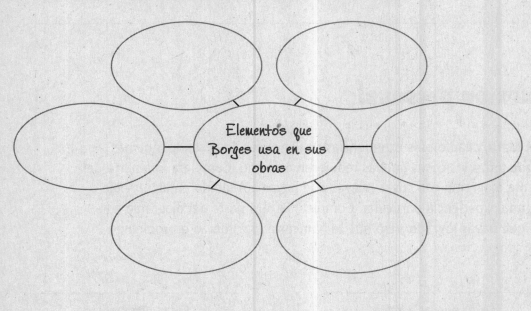

Elementos que Borges usa en sus obras

_____

_____

_____

What You Need to Know

Often, writers invent characters who narrate their stories in the first
person, but these characters are still fictional. One of the unusual
characteristics of Borges' literature is that he frequently included himself
as one of the main characters. When the other characters talk, they refer
to him simply as "Borges."

Jorge Luis Borges

Los laberintos y **sueños**, la fantasía, las identidades misteriosas y la suspensión del tiempo… todos son temas importantes en las obras de Jorge Luis Borges, uno de los autores

5 latinoamericanos más reconocidos del siglo XX.

Borges nació en Buenos Aires en 1899 y vivió allí hasta 1914. Comenzó a escribir a la edad de nueve años, cuando publicó una traducción al español del cuento *The Happy*

10 *Prince* de Oscar Wilde. Muchas de sus primeras lecturas fueron en inglés porque su hogar era bilingüe, ya que su abuela era inglesa. A los trece años, publicó su primer cuento original sobre tigres. Desde entonces,

15 los tigres fueron un símbolo importante en la obra de Borges.

PALABRAS CLAVE
el sueño *dream*

READING TIP This reading mentions different parts of the world that Borges lived in. To better understand how far he traveled and the different experiences he had, look at a map or an atlas to locate Argentina and its capital Buenos Aires, Switzerland, and Spain.

APUNTES

▥ MÁRCALO ▷ GRAMÁTICA
Review the forms and uses of the preterite and the imperfect. Then read the boxed text, underlining all the verbs in the preterite and circling all the verbs in the imperfect.

APUNTES

A pensar...

1. Make an X next to the sentences that describe Borges' writing. (**Connect**)

   a. Borges fundó revistas.

   b. Trató temas de la historia de su familia.

   c. Se mudó a Suiza.

   d. Libró batallas de la imaginación.

   e. Capturó la esencia de sí mismo.

2. Which of the following sets of words is associated with Borges' style? (**Clarify**)

   a. poemas, soldado, inglés

   b. tigres, Suiza, ficciones

   c. identidad, fantasía, misterio

   d. esencia, piedra, espada

En 1914, su familia se mudó a Suiza y en 1919, **se trasladó** a España, donde Borges publicó «Himno al mar», su primer poema en español.

20 Regresó a Buenos Aires en 1921, fundó revistas y publicó su primera colección de poemas, *Fervor de Buenos Aires* (1923). Publicó poesía a lo largo de[1] su vida.

Elogio de la sombra (1969), *El oro de los tigres*
25 (1972) y *La rosa profunda* (1975) son otros libros de poemas conocidos. En estos libros, Borges trata los temas de la historia de su familia, una que participó en varias etapas de la historia de Argentina. Su abuelo paterno participó en la
30 guerra civil de Argentina; su abuelo materno también fue soldado. Borges se veía muy distinto a ellos, como dice en «Soy», un poema de *La rosa profunda*:

    ❝ Soy... el que no fue una espada
35   **en la guerra. ❞**

_____
[1]throughout

PALABRAS CLAVE
trasladarse *to move*

Borges no luchó con una **espada** de verdad, pero libró batallas de la imaginación[2] que resultaron en una obra **voluminosa**. Además de poemas, publicó varias colecciones de

40 cuentos. Entre las más importantes se encuentran *Ficciones* (1944) y *El **Aleph*** (1949). En sus cuentos, Borges explora el límite entre la realidad y la fantasía y cómo a veces estas cosas se confunden en nuestras vidas.

45 El sentido del **ser** —quiénes somos y cómo formamos nuestra identidad— es otro de los temas importantes en la obra de Borges. Él veía su identidad como escritor aparte de su identidad como hombre. Pero Borges el

50 escritor es el que captura finalmente la **esencia** de Borges el hombre. Hablando de sí mismo como escritor dijo:

> 66 ...todas las cosas quieren perseverar en
> su ser[3]; la piedra eternamente quiere ser piedra
55 > y el tigre un tigre. Yo he de quedar en Borges,
> no en mí (si es que alguien soy)... 99

---

[2] fought battles of the imagination   [3] persevere in being themselves

CHALLENGE In the quoted text at the end of the reading, Borges compares himself to both a rock and a tiger. Why do you think he refers to something that is living and something that is not? (**Make Judgments**)

PALABRAS CLAVE
la espada   *sword*
voluminoso(a)   *voluminous*
el aleph   *first letter of the Hebrew alphabet*

el ser   *being*
la esencia   *essence*

Vocabulario de la lectura

Palabras clave

el aleph *first letter of the Hebrew alphabet*
la esencia *essence*
la espada *sword*
el ser *being*

el sueño *dream*
trasladarse *to move*
voluminoso(a) *voluminous*

A. Completa cada analogía con una **palabra clave.** En una analogía, las últimas dos palabras deben estar relacionadas de la misma manera que los primeras dos.

1. LIBRO : REVISTA :: revólver : _____

2. CONDUCIR : MANEJAR :: mudarse : _____

3. CONTENTO : TRISTE : pequeño : _____

4. LUNES : ENERO :: A : _____

5. MISTERIO : INTRIGA :: ilusión : _____

B. Completa cada oración con las **palabras clave** correctas. Escribe los verbos en su forma correcta. Debes usar cada **palabra clave** sólo una vez.

1. Borges vivía en Suiza con su familia y luego _____ a España.

2. Según sus propias palabras, Borges libró guerras sin _____.

3. En sus obras, Borges rescata su propia _____.

4. Los años de trabajo y su capacidad creativa produjeron una colección

   _____.

5. El _____ y la identidad es uno de los temas principales en la obra de Borges.

¿Comprendiste?

1. ¿Cómo comenzó la carrera literaria de Borges? ¿Qué lo hizo famoso?

_____

_____

2. ¿Cuáles son unos temas importantes de sus obras?

_____

_____

3. ¿Qué tipos de obras literarias escribió Borges? ¿Cómo es el estilo de Borges?

_____

_____

Conexión personal

Borges hizo su primera traducción a los nueve años de edad. ¿Crees que un niño tiene suficiente capacidad para hacer ese trabajo? ¿Conoces a alguien que haya hecho lo mismo? ¿Tú has hecho algo parecido cuando eras niño? Escribe tu opinión y tus experiencias en la libreta de la derecha.

En mi opinión...

_____

_____

_____

_____

_____

_____

_____

_____

_____

_____

_____

_____

Para leer   *Paula*

Reading Strategy

SPECULATE ABOUT THE AUTHOR From your reading, what do you
think was the age and professional status of Isabel Allende during her
career? What other activities does she reveal? Do you think it is better
to read a piece of literature with or without knowledge about the
author? Use the following chart to organize your ideas.

Isabel Allende		
Edad	**Actividad profesional**	**Otras actividades**
Mi opinión		

What You Need to Know

The 1960s gave rise to an important generation of Chilean journalists,
writers, artists, teachers, and other intellectuals, many of whom became
spokespersons for social reform. Under the dictatorship of Augusto
Pinochet, who seized power in a coup in 1973, many such intellectuals,
including Isabel Allende, were forced into exile.

Sobre la autora

Isabel Allende, novelista chilena, nació en Lima, Perú, en 1942. Su familia tuvo que exiliarse de Chile cuando su tío Salvador Allende, el presidente del país, fue vencido por una junta militar en 1973. Isabel Allende empezó a escribir a la edad de diecisiete años y escribió su primera novela, *La casa de los espíritus*, en 1982. También ha trabajado como periodista y en la televisión.

Introducción Allende comenzó a escribir su libro autobiográfico *Paula* mientras su hija estaba muy enferma. Es una historia que ofrece mucha información y varias anécdotas sobre la familia de Allende y sobre la historia y la política de Chile. En la selección que vas a leer, Allende le habla a su hija sobre su trabajo en Chile.

Paula

A comienzo de los años sesenta mi trabajo había progresado de las estadísticas forestales a unos **tambaleantes inicios** en el periodismo, que me condujeron por
5 casualidad a la televisión.

. . .

Fue así como terminé a cargo de un programa en el cual me tocaba hacer desde el **guión** hasta los dibujos de los créditos. El trabajo en el Canal consistía en llegar puntual, sentarme
10 ante una luz roja y hablar al vacío; nunca tomé conciencia de que al otro lado de la luz

PALABRAS CLAVE
tambaleante *shaky*
el inicio *beginning*
el guión *script*

APUNTES

READING TIP Note that Isabel Allende starts by talking about herself. Then, it becomes clear that she is addressing her daughter, Paula. Watch for verbs in the second person singular that indicate Allende is talking to Paula.

APUNTES

You have just reviewed the use of possessive pronouns. Find and circle all the possessive pronouns in the boxed text.

A pensar...

How did Paula react when she saw her mother in TV? Write several sentences using your own words. **(Analyze)**

_____

_____

_____

_____

_____

_____

_____

CHALLENGE Based on this selection, what do you think the relationship between Isabel and Paula was like? Do you think it was a good experience for Paula to see her mother on TV? Write your opinions and circle passages that support them. **(Evaluate)**

_____

_____

_____

_____

_____

_____

_____

_____

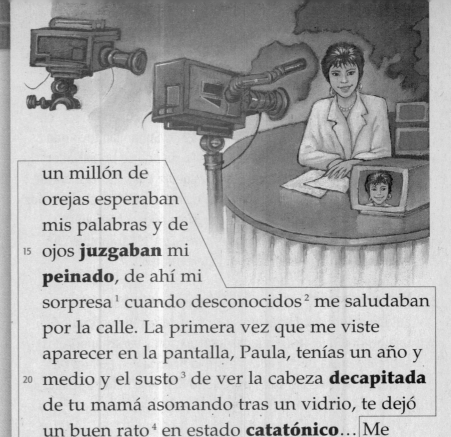

un millón de orejas esperaban mis palabras y de
15 ojos **juzgaban** mi **peinado**, de ahí mi sorpresa[1] cuando desconocidos[2] me saludaban por la calle. La primera vez que me viste aparecer en la pantalla, Paula, tenías un año y
20 medio y el susto[3] de ver la cabeza **decapitada** de tu mamá asomando tras un vidrio, te dejó un buen rato[4] en estado **catatónico**... Me convertí en la persona más **conspicua** del barrio, los vecinos me saludaban con respeto y
25 los niños me señalaban[5] con el dedo...
(Michael y yo) conseguimos un par de **becas**, partimos a Europa y llegamos a Suiza contigo de la mano, tenías casi dos años y eras una mujer en miniatura.

[1] surprise   [2] strangers   [3] shock, fright   [4] quite a while
[5] gestured to me

PALABRAS CLAVE

juzgar _to judge_	**conspicuo(a)** _conspicuous:_
el peinado _hairdo_	_noticeable, important_
decapitado(a) _decapitated_	**la beca** _scholarship_
catatónico(a) _catatonic_	

Vocabulario de la lectura

Palabras clave

la beca *scholarship*

catatónico(a) *catatonic*

conspicuo(a) *noticeable*

decapitado(a) *decapitated*

la estadística forestal *forestry statistics*

el guión *script*

el inicio *beginning*

juzgar *to judge*

el peinado *hairdo*

tambaleante *shaky*

A. Completa el siguiente párrafo con las **palabras clave** correctas. Luego ordena las letras que queden en las casillas para descubrir la palabra secreta.

Según Isabel Allende, sus primeros pasos en el mundo del periodismo fueron

___ ___ ___ ___ ___ □ ___ ___ ___ ___ ___ ___. Unos de sus trabajos era escribir

el ___ □ ___ ___ ___ para los programas. Cuando empezó a aparecer en

televisión, Isabel no se daba cuenta de que muchas personas se fijarían en su

□ ___ ___ ___ ___ ___ ___. Cuando su hijita vio la imagen de Isabel en la

televisión pensó que estaba ___ ___ ___ ___ ___ ___ ___ ___ ___ □. Tiempo

después, Isabel Allende consiguió algunas ___ ___ ___ □ ___ y partió a Europa.

□ □ □ □ □

B. Haz un círculo alrededor de la **palabra clave** entre paréntesis que mejor complete la oración.

1. Antes de trabajar en la televisión, Isabel Allende realizaba (estadísticas forestales / guiones)

2. En sus (inicios / becas) en el mundo del periodismo, pasó por varias etapas.

3. Desde que apareció en televisión, la gente la (decapitaba / juzgaba).

4. Debido a la reacción de la gente, Isabel se había convertido en una persona (conspicua / catatónica).

5. Paula se llevó una sorpresa tan grande al ver a su mamá en la pantalla, que quedó en estado (tambaleante / catatónico).

¿Comprendiste?

1. ¿En qué campos trabajaba Isabel Allende?

_____

2. ¿En qué consistía su trabajo en la televisión?

_____

3. ¿Por qué se fue la escritora de Chile?

_____

4. ¿De qué se trata el libro *Paula*?

_____

Conexión personal

¿Alguna vez has estado en un estudio de televisión? ¿Cómo te parece que sea la experiencia de que millones de personas vean tu cara en la pantalla y luego te reconozcan por la calle? ¿Cómo reaccionarías? ¿Cómo crees que te verían tus familiares y amigos? Escribe lo que piensas en la libreta de al lado.

Si yo saliera por televisión...

_____

_____

_____

_____

_____

_____

_____

_____

_____

_____

Para leer   *Miguel de Unamuno · Ana María Matute*

Reading Strategy

COMPARE FAMOUS AUTHORS Unamuno and Matute share a love of Spain. How else are they alike or different? Use this chart to make your comparisons. What emotions does each express in the excerpts you read?

	Unamuno	**Matute**
fechas importantes		
eventos influyentes		
preocupaciones		
emociones expresadas		

What You Need to Know

In February of 1936, after five years of political instability in Spain, a socialist government was elected, but political divisions remained within the country. Conflicts between opposing liberal and conservative factions eventually developed into the Spanish Civil War. General Francisco Franco, who fought against the socialists, took control of Spain after three years of war, beginning what was known as the Franquismo era. During his repressive dictatorship, which lasted more than 30 years, there was limited freedom of speech and freedom of the press. Many Spanish writers and artists faced the threat of censorship, exile, or execution.

READING TIP Biographical readings frequently contain quotations from the person being discussed. The quoted text is often preceded by a colon. Look for the quotations in this reading and highlight the sentences that introduce them.

A pensar...

1. Make a list of the five main topics that Miguel de Unamuno discussed in his works. **(Clarify)**

_____

_____

_____

_____

2. A paraphrase is a restatement of a text or passage in other words, often to clarify meaning. How would you paraphrase Unamuno's "Venceréis pero no convenceréis"? **(Paraphrase)**

_____

_____

_____

_____

_____

_____

_____

_____

Miguel de Unamuno

Miguel de Unamuno, escritor español, nació en Bilbao en 1864 y fue uno de los autores más importantes del siglo XIX. Tuvo una gran conciencia social y se preocupó mucho por
5 la identidad y el futuro de España, como otros autores de su generación, que se llama «La Generación del '98».

Unamuno además pensaba mucho sobre cuestiones filosóficas de la vida y de la
10 inmortalidad. **Cultivó** todos los géneros literarios, pero sus ensayos y novelas son los más famosos.

Unamuno escribió sobre su amor a España y los problemas políticos del país durante un
15 período de cambio violento. De él es la cita conocida:

> ❝ ¡Me duele España! ❞

PALABRAS CLAVE
cultivar _to cultivate_

Durante esa época, una guerra civil empezó en España. Unamuno se opuso a Francisco Franco, el general **derechista.** Por esto, las fuerzas de Franco mantuvieron a Unamuno bajo **arresto** a domicilio. Unamuno murió el último día de 1936 —el primer año de la guerra— sin cambiar su opinión política. Dijo:

25

" Venceréis pero no convenceréis. "

Ana María Matute

Ana María Matute, novelista española contemporánea, nació en Barcelona en 1926. Tenía diez años cuando comenzó la guerra civil y su familia se mudaba de Madrid a Barcelona para escaparse de la violencia.

PALABRAS CLAVE
el (la) derechista *member of the right wing*
el arresto *detention*
convencer *to convince*

APUNTES

APUNTES

_____

_____

_____

_____

_____

_____

_____

_____

CHALLENGE What elements do Unamuno's and Matute's life have in common? Who do you believe suffered most from the Spanish Civil War from an artistic point of view? Who suffered most from the consequences of the war? To which trauma does Matute refer in her quote? Do you think Unamuno experienced similar feelings? Write your ideas on the lines below. (Compare and Contrast)

_____

_____

_____

_____

_____

_____

_____

El punto de vista triste de sus novelas **refleja** la desilusión que ella sintió durante la guerra civil y los años de represión que la siguieron.

Ella dice:

35   ❝ **Todo era injusto e incomprensible. El mundo no era tal y como nos lo habían explicado. Yo creo que nuestra generación dio tantos grandes escritores porque fuimos víctimas de un trauma muy fuerte. No se podía hacer ni decir nada. De ahí nació un**
40   **sentimiento de rebeldía que creo aún mantengo.** ❞

A pesar de sus experiencias traumáticas de niña, Matute ha tenido un éxito extraordinario con su producción literaria. Además de ser una de los autoras más importantes de la narrativa
45   de **posguerra** española, es la única mujer en la Real Academia de España. Entre sus novelas más conocidas están _Los Abel, Los hijos muertos, La trampa, El río_ y _Olvidado Rey Gudú._

Ella reconoce la dificultad de escribir novelas.
50   Dice:

❝ **Quien diga lo contrario o miente, o es un genio, ¡o es un desastre!** ❞

PALABRAS CLAVE
reflejar   _to reflect_   **mentir**   _to lie_
la posguerra   _postwar_   **el genio**   _genius_

Vocabulario de la lectura

Palabras clave

el arresto *detention*
convencer *to convince*
cultivar *to cultivate*
el (la) derechista *member of the right wing*

el genio *genius*
mentir *to lie*
la posguerra *postwar*
reflejar *to reflect*

A. Elige la opción que explique correctamente cada oración.

1. Miguel de Unamuno estuvo bajo arresto domiciliario.
   a. Estuvo preso en una isla.
   b. Estuvo escribiendo mucho en su casa.
   c. Estuvo preso en su casa.

2. Unamuno cultivó todos los géneros literarios.
   a. Escribía en su jardín.
   b. Escribía en varios estilos.
   c. Rechazó muchos géneros literarios.

3. La tristeza de las novelas de Ana María Matute reflejan su desilusión.
   a. Matute no escribirá más.
   b. Quiere olvidar su desilusión.
   c. Quiere explicar su desilusión.

4. Ana María Matute es una escritora importante de la posguerra española.
   a. Escribió mucho después de la guerra.
   b. Escribió durante la guerra.
   c. Escribió principalmente antes de la guerra.

5. «Quien diga lo contrario, miente.»
   a. Lo contrario es la verdad.
   b. Lo contrario no es verdad.
   c. Lo contrario puede ser verdad.

B. Completa el párrafo con las **palabras clave** apropiadas. Escribe los verbos en su forma correcta.

Unamuno se opuso al régimen _____ de Franco. Él opinó que
                                        (1)
aunque los derechistas ganen la guerra no podrán _____ al pueblo.
                                                            (2)
En España, la _____ estuvo caracterizada por una dictadura. Matute
                        (3)
_____ en sus obras su tristeza por España. Según ella, los que dicen
         (4)
que escribir novelas es fácil, deben ser unos _____.
                                                        (5)

¿Comprendiste?

1. ¿A qué generación literaria pertenece Unamuno?

_____

2. ¿Cuál es la actitud de Unamuno hacia Francisco Franco y sus fuerzas?

_____

3. ¿Cómo influyó la guerra civil de España en el pensamiento y la vida de Matute?

_____

_____

4. Según Matute, ¿por qué hay tantos escritores buenos en su generación?

_____

Conexión personal

Si tú fueras un escritor y el país cayera en una dictadura, ¿cómo reaccionarías? ¿Seguirías escribiendo? ¿Tendrías miedo? ¿Cambiarías el tema de tu obra? ¿Te irías del país? Escribe tu punto de vista en la libreta de la derecha.

Pienso que...
_____
_____
_____
_____
_____
_____
_____
_____
_____
_____

Para leer   *La casa de Bernarda Alba*

Reading Strategy

INTERPRET A DRAMA Reading a play requires the interpretation of characters, their motivations, even their movements and gestures. In a novel those elements are often described. Imagine yourself as the director of *La casa de Bernarda Alba*. First read the entire scene; then read the lines of each character separately, ignoring all others. How would you advise each actress to play her role?

Cómo hacer el papel de…	
Magdalena	
Martirio	
Amelia	

What You Need to Know

Note that García Lorca's *La casa de Bernarda Alba* has a subtitle–*Drama de mujeres en los pueblos de España. Pueblos* is a significant word in the subtitle, because this play is about life in a small village. In order to understand this selection better, it is important to know that in the small towns of Europe in the 1800s, it was an aspiration of many women to be married at an early age.

A pensar...

Who is going to get married? Who are Martirio, Amelia, and Magdalena? Where do they live? What is Martirio's opinion of Pepe el Romano? **(Clarify)**

Sobre el autor

Federico García Lorca nació en Granada en 1898. Vivió durante la Guerra Civil en España, período turbulento, y murió a manos del ejército del General Francisco Franco. García Lorca es famoso por su poesía lírica y sus obras teatrales. Tal vez sea mejor conocido por su gran trilogía de dramas: *Bodas de sangre, Yerma* y *La casa de Bernarda Alba.*

Introducción *La casa de Bernarda Alba,* Drama de mujeres en los pueblos de España, tiene tres actos. Vas a leer unas líneas de una escena del primer acto. Tres hijas de Bernarda Alba discuten sobre el pretendiente de su hermana Angustias. Hablan Magdalena, que tiene 30 años, Martirio, de 24 años y Amelia, de 27 años.

La casa de Bernarda Alba

MAGDALENA ¡Ah! Ya se comenta por el pueblo. Pepe el Romano viene a casarse con Angustias. Anoche estuvo **rondando** la casa y creo que pronto va a mandar un **emisario.**

5 MARTIRIO Yo me alegro. Es buen mozo.

AMELIA Yo también. Angustias tiene buenas condiciones.

MAGDALENA Ninguna de las dos os alegráis.

PALABRAS CLAVE
rondar *to hang around*   **el (la) emisario(a)** *emissary*

READER'S
SUCCESS
STRATEGY Reread the
introduction to this selection.
Pay attention to the ages of
the three sisters and evaluate
if this information is
important for the plot of
the drama.

APUNTES

10 MARTIRIO ¡Magdalena! ¡Mujer!

> MAGDALENA Si viniera por el tipo de
> Angustias, por Angustias como mujer, yo me
> alegraría; pero viene por el dinero. Aunque
> Angustias es nuestra hermana, aquí estamos
> 15 en familia y reconocemos que está vieja,
> **enfermiza,** y que siempre ha sido la que ha
> tenido menos méritos de todas nosotras.

Porque si con veinte años parecía un palo[1]
vestido, ¡qué será ahora que tiene cuarenta!

[1] stick

MÁRCALO GRAMÁTICA
You have learned how to use
the relative pronoun **que** to
provide additional information.
In the boxed text, find and
circle the relative pronoun.

PALABRAS CLAVE
enfermizo(a) *sickly*

CHALLENGE In the first act of this drama, you learned that the three sisters have different points of view about Angustias. Do you think this situation will generate conflicts within the family? If so, what kinds of problems do you think they will have to face? How do you think Pepe el Romano will react? (**Predict**)

20 MARTIRIO No hables así. La suerte viene a quien menos la **aguarda**.

AMELIA ¡Después de todo dice la verdad! ¡Angustias tiene todo el dinero de su padre, es la única rica de la casa y por eso ahora que
25 nuestro padre ha muerto y ya se harán **particiones** viene por ella!

MAGDALENA Pepe el Romano tiene veinticinco años y es el mejor tipo de todos estos **contornos**. Lo natural sería que te
30 **pretendiera** a ti, Amelia, o a nuestra Adela, que tiene veinte años, pero no que venga a buscar lo más **oscuro** de esta casa, a una mujer que, como su padre, habla con las narices.

MARTIRIO ¡Puede que a él le guste!

35 MAGDALENA ¡Nunca he podido resistir[2] tu hipocresía!

---

[2] to stand, put up with

PALABRAS CLAVE

aguardar	*to expect*	**pretender**	*to be a suitor for*
la partición	*division*	**oscuro(a)**	*dark; the least desirable (fig.)*
los contornos	*surroundings*		

Vocabulario de la lectura

Palabras clave

aguardar *to expect*

los contornos *surroundings*

el (la) emisario(a) *emissary*

enfermizo(a) *sickly*

oscuro(a) *dark; the least desirable (fig.)*

la partición *division*

pretender *to be a suitor for*

rondar *to hang around*

A. Reemplaza la palabra subrayada con una **palabra clave** apropiada y escríbela en la línea que figura al lado. Escribe los verbos en su forma correcta.

1. El <u>mensajero</u> le entregó una carta al capitán. _____

2. Dos ladrones estaban <u>caminando</u> cerca de la casa de Elena. _____

3. Mateo sempre se siente mal. Es una persona muy <u>delicada</u>. _____

4. El juez llamó a toda la familia para hacer la <u>separación</u> de la herencia.

   _____

5. Los <u>alrededores</u> de la mansión están bien vigilados por la policía.

   _____

B. Completa el siguiente párrafo con las **palabras clave** correctas.
Escribe los verbos en su forma apropiada.

Cerca de la casa de Bernarda Alba _____ Pepe el Romano, quien
                                            (1)

_____ a una de sus hijas. Según Magdalena, otra hija de Bernarda,
        (2)

Pepe era el hombre más atractivo de esos _____ y le parecía raro
                                                  (3)

que él estuviera interesado en una persona tan _____ como su
                                                      (4)

hermana. Y según Martirio, otra hermana más, los pretendientes llegan cuando

menos se los _____ .
                  (5)

¿Comprendiste?

1. ¿Cuál es la actitud de cada una de las hermanas en cuanto al novio de Angustias?

_____

_____

2. ¿Quién es Adela? ¿Cuántos años tiene? ¿Quién es Pepe el Romano?

_____

_____

3. ¿Cómo es Angustias, según Magdalena?

_____

_____

Conexión personal

¿Estás de acuerdo con la opinión de Magdalena con respecto a las intenciones de Pepe? ¿Cómo comprobarías tú cuáles son sus verdaderos propósitos? ¿Qué pruebas le harías a una persona para saber si realmente está interesado en ti o en tu dinero? Completa la siguiente tabla con oraciones que resuman tus ideas.

Prueba de honestidad
Actitudes sospechosas:
Actitudes honestas:
Prueba N° 1:
Prueba N° 2:
Solución:

Para leer   *Brillo afuera, oscuridad en casa*

Reading Strategy

DISTINGUISH FACTS FROM INTERPRETATIONS Magazine articles
offer both factual information and the author's interpretations.
Based on your reading of *Brillo afuera, oscuridad en casa*, decide
which of these statements are fact and which are interpretation.
Use the text of the article to justify your choices.

Información de la lectura	Hecho	Interpretación
El autor representa una perspectiva venezolana.		
«Amor mío» es más popular en EE.UU. que en Venezuela.		
La población hispana en EE.UU. ha aumentado. Por eso, la popularidad de programas hispanos ha aumentado también.		
Tres programas venezolanos están entre los diez primeros espacios en popularidad.		
Es mejor tener éxito internacional que éxito local.		

What You Need to Know

Soap operas are very popular in Latin America. Countries like Venezuela,
Mexico, Colombia, and Argentina have produced an endless number of
titles that have lasted in the memory of the audience for years. Typical
themes in Latin American soap operas are love, family conflicts, wealth and
poverty. In many cases these topics alternate with politics and detective
situations, to give a touch of mystery and suspense. Many of these soap
operas have been rebroadcast on Spanish channels in the United States.
Many others have been exported to Europe, where they are dubbed into
other languages. In the last few years, TV channels in Miami have started
their own local production of soap operas with Latino actors, many of
whom have already appeared in Hollywood movies.

READING TIP Generally, articles in magazines start with a title, followed by a paragraph in italics or a different font from the one used in the main text of the article. These paragraphs work as an introduction and are written in a way to catch the interest of the reader so that he or she keeps reading the whole article. Find the introductory paragraph in the article to see if it catches your attention.

APUNTES

Farándula es una revista sobre la programación de televisión en Venezuela. Esta revista también ofrece artículos sobre actores populares de América Latina, Estados Unidos y Europa.

Introducción Vas a leer un artículo sobre una telenovela que se llama «Amor mío», uno de los programas de origen venezolano más populares en Estados Unidos.

Brillo afuera, oscuridad en casa

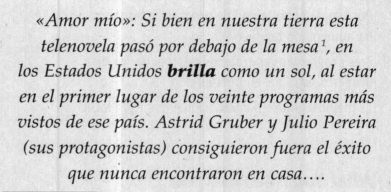

«Amor mío»: Si bien en nuestra tierra esta telenovela pasó por debajo de la mesa[1], en los Estados Unidos **brilla** como un sol, al estar en el primer lugar de los veinte programas más vistos de ese país. Astrid Gruber y Julio Pereira (sus protagonistas) consiguieron fuera el éxito que nunca encontraron en casa....

5

[1] went unnoticed

PALABRAS CLAVE
brillar   *to shine*

MÁRCALO ▷ GRAMÁTICA
Note that most of this article is written in the present tense. However, there is a part with verbs in the preterite to explain what happened before the article. Find and circle the verbs in the preterite.

$\heartsuit$ **L**os programas de habla hispana son cada
   vez más populares en Estados Unidos. Al
10 parecer, la **creciente** población latina de ese
   país es la razón principal. Pero lo importante
   de todo esto es que en esta área le llevamos
   ventaja a muchas naciones, pues nuestra
   televisión es una de las más vistas.

15 Es así como en los actuales momentos, según
   el *ranking* que incluyen los veinte primeros
   espacios[2] de la televisión **emanados** de la
   Nielsen Hispanic Televisión, tenemos tres
   muy buenas posiciones. «Sábado sensacional»,
20 por su parte, ocupa el puesto número siete,
   «Maite» está en el puesto tres y, como gran
   victoria, encontramos a la novela «Amor mío»
   en el primer lugar.

   Sus protagonistas, Astrid Gruber y Julio
25 Pereira, son **idolatrados** (como nunca aquí)
   en los Estados Unidos al igual que los
   creadores del **dramático** que son Isamar
   Hernández, Ricardo García y Manuel
   Manzano.

30 Ahora sí pueden cantar victoria y no pasar
   por debajo de la mesa. Por tanto,
   demostramos que, una vez más, existe brillo
   afuera y oscuridad en casa.

PALABRAS CLAVE

creciente *growing*	**idolatrado(a)** *idolized*
el espacio *television program*	**el dramático** *soap opera*
emanado(a) *emanated, sent forth*	

A pensar...

Which of the following sentences best describes the main message in the article? (**Identify Main Idea and Details**)

1. Latin American soap operas are more popular than European soap operas.
2. The Hispanic population in the U.S. is growing fast.
3. Latin American soap operas are very successful in the U.S.
4. Venezuela is the country with the highest production of soap operas.

CHALLENGE Why do you think the article states that this soap opera went unnoticed in Venezuela but was very popular in the United States? What makes a foreign production attractive to Americans? Why do you think the soap opera actors don't reach the same level of fame in their native countries? (**Infer**)

_____

_____

_____

_____

_____

Vocabulario de la lectura

Palabras clave

brillar   *to shine*

creciente   *growing*

el dramático   *soap opera*

emanado(a)   *emanated, sent forth*

el espacio   *television program*

idolatrado(a)   *idolized*

A. Empareja cada **palabra clave** con la definición correcta. En la línea que figura al lado de cada palabra, escribe la letra correspondiente a la definición de dicha palabra.

_____ 1. creciente

_____ 2. idolatrado

_____ 3. brillar

_____ 4. espacio

_____ 5. dramático

A. figurativamente, tener éxito

B. cada uno de los lugares que ocupa cada programa de televisión

C. que aumenta

D. otro nombre para «novela»

E. muy famoso y querido

B. Completa los espacios en blanco con la **palabra clave** apropiada. Escribe los verbos en su forma correcta. Solamente puedes usar cada palabra una vez.

La revista *Farándula* se especializa en los _____ (1) de televisión venezolanos. En su artículo dice que la _____ (2) población latina de Estados Unidos está muy entusiasmada con los programas de Venezuela _____ (3) de las cadenas latinas, y que sus actores son _____ (4) por el público. Según la revista, las telenovelas venezolanas _____ (5) como un sol.

¿Comprendiste?

1. ¿por qué son cada vez más populares en Estados Unidos los programas en español?

_____

2. ¿Qué programas venezolanos son más populares entre los televidentes hispanos? ¿Cómo lo sabes?

_____

_____

3. Según el artículo, el éxito de «Amor mío» demuestra que «existe brillo afuera y oscuridad en casa». ¿Qué quiere decir?

_____

_____

Conexión personal

¿Qué opinión tienes sobre la programación en español en Estados Unidos? ¿Crees que se podría mejorar? ¿Qué otros temas se deberían tocar? Si estuvieras a cargo de la programación, ¿qué programas cambiarías y cuáles dejarías? Haz una lista con tus ideas.

La televisión en EE.UU.

_____

_____

_____

_____

_____

_____

_____

_____

_____

Para leer *Gabriel García Márquez*

Reading Strategy

MONITOR COMPREHENSION A good self-check is to restate (paraphrase) what each paragraph is about with a phrase or short sentence. If you can't, then reread, identify what seems unclear, and ask questions. Jot down a brief paraphrase of each paragraph as you read. You can then use those notes to write a brief summary about **el autor, su vida y su obra.** This will help you start:

1. La lectura empieza con una cita de una novela de García Márquez.
2.
3.
4.
5.

What You Need to Know

The term "magical realism" was first introduced by Franz Roh, a German art critic, who considered magical realism an art category. In Latin America in the 1940s, magical realism was a new way to express the reality and create a new style of literature. Time is one of the main themes, which is frequently displayed as cyclical instead of linear. In other words, what happens once is destined to happen again. Magical realist authors in Latin America include Gabriel García Márquez, Isabel Allende, Alejo Carpentier, and Mario Vargas Llosa.

Gabriel García Márquez

" Muchos años después, ante el pelotón de fusilamiento[1], el coronel Aureliano Buendía había de recordar aquella tarde remota en que su padre lo llevó a conocer el hielo[2]. "

Así comienza *Cien años de soledad* (1967), la novela más conocida de Gabriel García Márquez, uno de los escritores principales de las Américas en el siglo XX. Se ha dicho
5 que dentro de la literatura latinoamericana, *Cien años de soledad* tiene tanta importancia como *El Quijote* de Cervantes.

Como en muchas de las obras de García Márquez, esta novela **entreteje** las historias
10 de individuos con la historia de su pueblo. En *Cien años de soledad,* el pueblo es Macondo y los individuos son los miembros de la familia Buendía. García Márquez narra los **acontecimientos** de la historia del pueblo y
15 de la familia Buendía utilizando un estilo conocido como realismo mágico. Este estilo combina la realidad con elementos fantásticos.

[1] firing squad   [2] ice

PALABRAS CLAVE
remoto(a) *remote*   **el acontecimiento** *event*
entretejer *to interweave*

A pensar...

Connect the words that are related according to the reading. **(Clarify)**

Aureliano Buendía
Cien años de soledad
fantástico
García Márquez
Cervantes
novela
Macondo
mágico

APUNTES

MÁRCALO GRAMÁTICA
You have learned that many
verbs require the use of
prepositions. Read the boxed
text and circle those verbs
and the prepositions that
follow them.

APUNTES

El escritor insiste en que el realismo mágico
no es una combinación de elementos reales
20 y fantásticos, sino que es la manera en que
sucede la vida **cotidiana** de Colombia.
García Márquez nació en ese país en 1928 y
se **crió** con sus abuelos hasta la edad de ocho
años. Los cuentos que le hacía su abuela
25 influyeron sus escritos.

Cuando era joven, García Márquez se dedicó
al periodismo. Publicó su primera novela,
La hojarasca, en 1955. En *El coronel no tiene
quien le escriba* (1957), García Márquez siguió
30 utilizando la historia de Colombia como
marco de referencia para sus protagonistas.
Su fama aumentó con *El otoño del patriarca*
(1975) y *Crónica de una muerte anunciada* (1981).
En 1982, García Márquez ganó el Premio
35 Nóbel de Literatura. Continúa escribiendo
novelas y guiones para películas.

PALABRAS CLAVE
cotidiano(a) *daily*   **el marco** *frame*
criarse *to be raised*

CHALLENGE According to the last paragraph, what is the reaction of readers to García Márquez's works? What does the article mean with the phrase "Nuestra inquietud no es confusión"? What does García Márquez expect from his readers? (Infer)

Sin duda, García Márquez es una de las voces
más **potentes** de América Latina. Su visión
sugiere que el individuo es protagonista de
40 dos historias: la de su vida y la de su pueblo.
Al leer la obra de García Márquez, vemos que
a veces no es fácil saber dónde comienza una
historia y termina la otra. Nuestra **inquietud**
no es confusión, sin embargo: es el comienzo
45 de la **búsqueda** intrépida de quiénes somos y
seremos en el lugar donde nos ha tocado
vivir[3], sea en Macondo o Main Street.

[3] where it is our fate to live

PALABRAS CLAVE
potente *powerful*   **la búsqueda** *search*
la inquietud *uneasiness, anxiety*

Vocabulario de la lectura

Palabras clave

el acontecimiento *event*   **criarse** *to be raised*   **el marco** *frame*

la búsqueda *search*   **entretejer** *to interweave*   **potente** *powerful*

cotidiano(a) *daily*   **la inquietud** *uneasiness, anxiety*   **remoto(a)** *remote*

A. Completa el siguiente párrafo sobre la vida de Gabriel García Márquez con las **palabras clave** correctas. Luego ordena las letras que queden en las casillas para descubrir la palabra secreta.

1. García Márquez se □ __ __ __ con sus abuelos.

2. El __ □ __ __ __ de referencia de sus obras es la historia de Colombia.

3. El autor utiliza el realismo mágico para enfocarse en cosas

   __ □ __ __ __ __ __ __ __ __ .

4. Su característica es __ □ __ __ __ __ __ __ __ __ historias

   personales con la historia de su pueblo.

5. Generalmente sus obras causan una sensación de

   __ __ __ __ __ __ __ □ en el lector.

Palabra secreta: M __ __ __ __ o

B. Escoge la opción que mejor se asocie con la **palabra clave**.

1. acontecimiento
   a. pasado
   b. problema
   c. suceso

2. potente
   a. pesado
   b. débil
   c. poderoso

3. inquietud
   a. ansiedad
   b. traquilidad
   c. miedo

4. búsqueda
   a. investigación
   b. pérdida
   c. transporte

5. remoto
   a. mágico
   b. lejano
   c. real

¿Comprendiste?

1. ¿Quiénes son los protagonistas de *Cien años de soledad*? ¿Dónde sucede?

_____

_____

2. ¿Qué es el realismo mágico? ¿Qué combina?

_____

_____

3. ¿Qué influencia de la niñez de García Márquez aparece en sus obras?

_____

_____

4. ¿Qué papel juega la historia de un pueblo en la obra de García Márquez?

_____

Conexión personal

Según la lectura, existe una fuerte conexión entre la vida de una persona y la manera en que transcurre la realidad de la ciudad o pueblo donde vive. Di si estás de acuerdo y menciona algunos ejemplos de experiencias personales que estén ligadas a la manera en que se vive en tu ciudad. Si no estás de acuerdo, expone tus razones.

Creo que...

_____

_____

_____

_____

_____

_____

_____

_____

_____

_____

Literary Terms

alliteration   repetition of the same sounds in a phrase or a line of poetry

Anglicismo   use of English words in another language

antithesis   contrast between a word or a phrase and another that means the opposite

catalog   list of people, things, or attributes in a narration or poem

character   person in a literary work

flashback   scene from the past that interrupts the ongoing action of a work

hyperbole   exaggerated description of a person or thing

irony   contrast between what is stated and what is meant or between what is expected and what actually happens

metaphor   direct comparison between two unlike things

onomatopoeia   use of words to imitate the sound of something

parallelism   related ideas phrased in similar ways

personification   use of human characteristics to describe an animal or an object

protagonist   main character of a work

repetition   recurring sounds, words, or phrases to give emphasis

rhetorical question   interrogative sentence to which no answer is expected

rhyme   repetition of the same sound at the end of lines in a poem

rhyme pattern   repetition of rhyming sound at the end of alternating lines of a poem (ABAB, ABBA, or AABB, for example)

sensory details   descriptive words that appeal to the senses (sight, hearing, smell, taste, touch)

simile   comparison that uses *like* or *as*

Literatura adicional

En esta sección vas a encontrar una selección de lecturas literarias en español. Hay poemas, partes de novelas, ensayos y cuentos. Cada lectura tiene una biografía del autor e información relacionada con el tema de la selección. Como las lecturas de **En voces,** las lecturas literarias presentan estrategias, consejos y apoyo para la lectura, preguntas para razonar, actividades para practicar el vocabulario, preguntas de comprensión y una actividad de escritura, que te ayudarán a entender cada selección. También encontrarás la sección **Márcalo,** que te servirá para hacer el análisis literario de las lecturas.

Para leer   *Bendíceme, Última*

Reading Strategy

EVALUATE THE STORY When you **evaluate** a story, you make a judgment about it. Use this diagram to record your opinions on the setting, plot, characters, and theme of the story. Are they believable? Are they interesting? Support your opinions. Be sure your ideas are based on information in the story as well as in your own knowledge.

Ambiente	**Personajes**

Bendíceme, Última

Trama	**Tema**

What You Need to Know

Herbal healing is a very popular practice in Latin American countries, which includes the use of herbs, massages, and rituals to cure people. The theory of this practice says that there are people with the ability to apply the power of those herbs. Many stories have been written about herbal healers, and it is common to find these people, particularly in rural areas. Although it is true that many plants have curative properties, in many cases the likelihood of being cured depends largely on the beliefs of the individual person. In *Bendíceme, Última*, Rudolfo Anaya tells the story of a healer and her relationship with a family in New Mexico.

Sobre el autor

Rudolfo Anaya nació en Nuevo México en 1937. A través de sus novelas interpreta la vida de los hispanos en Estados Unidos, por eso se ha convertido en uno de los escritores hispanos más destacados de este país. En 1972 ganó el Premio Quinto Sol por su primera novela, *Bendíceme, Última*, y desde 1974 ha sido profesor de la Universidad de Nuevo México. Anaya usa su herencia chicana como fuente de inspiración, combinando la mitología de los mestizos, la importancia de la tierra nativa, la familia chicana y su vida en los Estados Unidos.

~~~~~~~~~~

Bendíceme, Última

Durante los últimos días de verano hay un tiempo en que lo maduro del otoño llena el aire. El tiempo transcurre[1] callado y suave y yo lo vivía con toda el alma, extrañamente
5   consciente de un nuevo mundo que se abría y tomaba forma sólo para mí. En las mañanas, antes de que hiciera mucho calor, Última y yo caminábamos por las **lomas** del **llano,** recogiendo las hierbas silvestres y raíces que
10 usaba para sus medicinas. Vagábamos[2] por los campos e íbamos de arriba abajo por el río. Yo cargaba una pequeña pala para **escarbar,** y ella una bolsa para guardar nuestra mágica cosecha.

---

[1] passes   [2] We wandered

PALABRAS CLAVE
   la loma *hill*   **escarbar** *to dig*
   el llano *plain*

READING TIP As you read *Bendíceme, Última*, try to imagine living in the place the writer describes.
  Look for details about Última's appearance and pay particular attention to the descriptions of the area.

APUNTES

READER'S SUCCESS STRATEGY Highlight the phrases that indicate how careful Última is with the herbs. Then, with a partner, read these lines aloud.

APUNTES

_____

_____

_____

_____

_____

_____

_____

_____

_____

A pensar...

Make a check mark next to the sentences that explain the relationship between Última and the narrator. **(Clarify)**

a. El tiempo transcurre callado y suave y yo lo vivía con toda el alma.

b. Luego escarbaba para sacar la planta con cuidado para no tocar sus raíces con la pala.

c. Yo repetia sus palabras tras ella.

d. Curaba quemaduras, ámpulas, problemas estomacales...

15 —¡Ay! —gritaba Última cuando descubría alguna planta o raíz que necesitaba—, cuánta suerte tenemos hoy para encontrar la hierba del **manso.**

Entonces me guiaba a la planta que sus ojos
20 de **lechuza** habían descubierto y me pedía que observara dónde crecía la planta y cómo eran sus hojas. —Ahora tócala —me decía—. Sus hojas son muy lisas y el color es verde muy claro.

25 Para Última, aun las plantas tenían alma, y antes de escarbar con la pala, me pedía que le hablara a la planta y le dijera por qué era necesario arrancarla de su hogar en la tierra. «Tú creces bien aquí en el arroyo junto a la
30 humedad del río, pero te alzamos para hacer una buena medicina» —entonaba suavemente Última, y yo repetía sus palabras tras ella. Luego escarbaba para sacar la planta con cuidado para no tocar sus raíces con la pala y
35 para no dañarlas. De todas las plantas que juntábamos, ninguna ofrecía tanta magia como la hierba del manso. Curaba quemaduras, ámpulas³, problemas estomacales, cólicos de recién nacido, disentería con sangre y hasta
40 reumatismo. Yo conocía esta planta de tiempo atrás, porque mi madre, que indudablemente no era **curandera,** la usaba con frecuencia.

³blisters

PALABRAS CLAVE
el manso _farmhouse_   el (la) curandero(a) _healer_
la lechuza _owl_

Las suaves manos de Última levantaban
cuidadosamente la planta y entonces la
45 examinaba. Tomaba una **pizca** y probaba su
calidad. Luego la metía en una pequeña bolsa
negra que traía colgando del cinturón. Me
había dicho que el contenido seco de la bolsita
era de una pizca de cada planta que ella había
50 recogido desde que empezó su entrenamiento
como curandera muchos años atrás.

> —Hace mucho tiempo —se sonreía—, mucho
> antes de que tú fueras un sueño, mucho antes
> de que el tren llegara a Las Pasturas, antes de
> 55 que los Luna llegaran al valle, antes de que el
> gran Coronado construyera el puente…
> —entonces su voz se iba por un sendero y mis
> pensamientos se perdían en el laberinto de un
> tiempo y una historia que no conocía.

60 Si en nuestra vagancia encontrábamos algo de
orégano recogíamos bastante no sólo porque
curaba tos y fiebre, sino porque mi madre lo
usaba como **especia** para sazonar[4] los frijoles
y la carne. También teníamos la suerte de
65 encontrar algo de *oshá*, planta que crece mejor
en las montañas y, como la hierba del manso,
lo cura todo. Cura la tos y los resfriados, las
cortadas y los raspones, el reumatismo y los
problemas estomacales. Mi padre dijo alguna
70 vez que los pastores[5] de ovejas la usaban para

---

[4] to flavor   [5] shepherds

PALABRAS CLAVE
la pizca *pinch*   **la especia** *aromatic herb*

CHALLENGE Why do you think the narrator enjoys his outings with Última? What is the new world that he refers to? Is there any indication in the reading that the reality of the narrator might be problematic? What do you think the environment in which the narrator lives is like? (**Make Judgments**)

_____

_____

_____

_____

_____

_____

_____

A pensar...

According to the narrator, each herb has different properties. In the space below, list some of the benefits provided by herbs and indicate which of these benefits is the most important to Última. (**Summarize**)

_____

_____

_____

_____

_____

_____

_____

mantener alejadas a las serpientes venenosas de los rollos de cobertores[6] para dormir. Sólo había que espolvorear[7] las frazadas con polvo de *oshá*. Con una mezcla de *oshá* Última había
75 lavado mi cara, mis brazos y pies, la noche que mataron a Lupito.

En las lomas, Última era feliz. Había una nobleza en su andar que le otorgaba gracia a su figura tan pequeña. La observaba
80 cuidadosamente y le imitaba el caminar, entonces sentía que ya no me perdería en el enorme paisaje del llano y del cielo. Yo era una parte muy importante en la palpitante vida del llano y del río.

85 —¡Mira! Qué suerte tenemos, hay **tunas** —gritó Última alegremente y apuntó a las tunas maduras y rojas del nopal—. Ven y recoge algunas para comerlas en la sombra del río —corrí al cactus y reuní una pala llena de
90 suculentas tunas llenas de semillas. Luego nos sentamos bajo la sombra de los álamos del río y pelamos las tunas con cuidado, porque aun en la piel tienen partes con pelusa[8] que irritan los dedos y la lengua. Comimos y nos
95 refrescamos.

_____

[6] blankets   [7] to sprinkle   [8] down

PALABRAS CLAVE
la tuna *a kind of tropical cactus*

Vocabulario de la lectura

Palabras clave

el (la) curandero(a) *healer*	**la lechuza** *owl*	**el manso** *farmhouse*
escarbar *to dig*	**el llano** *plain*	**la pizca** *pinch*
la especia *aromatic herb*	**la loma** *hill*	**la tuna** *a kind of tropical cactus*

A. Empareja cada **palabra clave** con la definición correcta. En la línea que figura al lado de cada palabra, escribe la letra correspondiente a la definición de dicha palabra.

_____ 1. pizca   A. elevación del terreno

_____ 2. lechuza   B. animal nocturno

_____ 3. loma   C. hacer un pozo en la tierra

_____ 4. curandera   D. un poquito

_____ 5. escarbar   E. mujer que cura con hierbas

B. Completa los espacios en blanco con la **palabra clave** correcta. Escribe los verbos en su forma correcta. Solamente puedes usar cada palabra una vez.

Última siempre salía a caminar por el _____ a buscar hierbas.
                                                       (1)

Con una pala _____ la tierra y decía que las hierbas
                             (2)

del _____ eran muy útiles. Algunas servían para curar y otras servían
                 (3)

como _____ para cocinar. Pero lo que más le gustaba encontrar
                     (4)

eran _____, pues éstas se podían comer a la orilla del río y eran
                  (5)

muy sabrosas.

¿Comprendiste?

1. ¿Quién es Última y qué actividades hace con el narrador del cuento?

_____

_____

2. ¿Qué tipo de consejos le da Última al narrador?

_____

_____

3. ¿Hace cuánto que Última es curandera?

_____

_____

4. ¿Qué sabe Última sobre la familia del narrador?

_____

_____

5. ¿Quiénes más confían en las hierbas que junta Última?

_____

_____

Conexión personal

¿Crees en las propiedades curativas de las hierbas? Justifica tu respuesta. Si alguna vez tú o alguien que conoces las ha usado, explica cuál era el problema y di si las hierbas lo han solucionado. Escribe tus comentarios en la libreta de la derecha.

Para mí, las hierbas...

_____

_____

_____

_____

_____

_____

_____

Para leer   *Canción de otoño en primavera*

Reading Strategy

CLARIFY THE MEANING OF POETRY The process of stopping
while reading to quickly review what has happened and to look
for answers to questions you may have is **clarifying**.
Complete the chart below by doing the following:

- Read the first two stanzas of "Canción de otoño en primavera."
- Stop to clarify those lines.
- In the first box, explain what happens in the lines you read.
- Read the next two stanzas and repeat the process.
- Read two more stanzas and complete the chart.

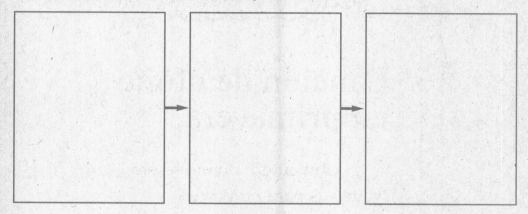

What You Need to Know

Many people, at a certain age, think of the balance in their lives. At that
moment, they make a summary of the good and bad things that they have
lived, including emotional and professional achievements. Poets often
show this balance in their works. Some of them tell their experiences in an
optimistic way, others with humor, and others with a lot of sadness
because of the things they lost. In «Canción de otoño en primavera»
Rubén Darío remembers the hopes and disappointments he had in his
youth in a very particular way.

READING TIP The poem in this selection is about past romantic relationships. As you read, look for clues that will help you understand the author's feelings. Think about the mood or atmosphere created by the author's descriptions.

APUNTES

Sobre el autor

Rubén Darío (1867–1916) nació en Metapa, Nicaragua. Desde joven se dedicó a leer obras de poetas franceses, que influenciaron su estilo. Rubén Darío es la figura principal del *modernismo,* un movimiento que renovó la literatura hispanoamericana. Desde niño manifestó una gran capacidad para la escritura; desde los once años de edad comenzó a componer versos y se lo conoció como «el niño poeta». Vivió también en Chile, Argentina y Francia, y trabajó como corresponsal de periódicos durante la Guerra Hispanoamericana. Entre sus obras se destacan *Azul* y *Cantos de vida y esperanza.* A esta última obra pertenece el poema «Canción de otoño en primavera».

Canción de otoño en primavera

Juventud, divino tesoro,
¡ya te vas para no volver!
Cuando quiero llorar, no lloro . . .
y a veces lloro sin querer.

5   Plural ha sido la **celeste**
historia de mi corazón.
Era una dulce niña, en este
mundo de **duelo** y aflicción.

PALABRAS CLAVE
celeste *celestial*   **el duelo** *mourning*

Miraba como el **alba** pura;
10 sonreía como una flor.
Era su cabellera obscura
hecha de noche y de dolor.

Yo era tímido como un niño.
Ella, naturalmente, fue,
15 para mi amor hecho de **armiño,**
Herodías[1] y Salomé[2] . . .

Juventud, divino tesoro,
¡ya te vas para no volver . . . !
Cuando quiero llorar, no lloro,
20 y a veces lloro sin querer . . .

La otra fue más sensitiva,
y más consoladora y más
halagadora y expresiva,
cual no pensé encontrar jamás.

25 Pues a su continua ternura
una pasión violenta unía.
En un **peplo** de **gasa** pura
una bacante[3] se envolvía . . .

---

[1] A Jewish princess who ordered the death of John the Baptist.
[2] She received John the Baptist's head.
[3] from Bacchus, a Greek god of festivity and celebration

APUNTES

A pensar...

Remember that a paraphrase is a restatement of a text or passage in other words, often to clarify meaning. How would you paraphrase Rubén Darío's «Juventud, divino tesoro, ¡ya te vas para no volver!»? **(Paraphrase)**

PALABRAS CLAVE

el alba *(fem.)* *dawn*
el armiño *ermine; soft fur*
halagador(a) *flattering*

el peplo *peplum, Roman tunic*
la gasa *gauze*

CHALLENGE Compare the three loves that Rubén Darío describes. What were the characteristics of each one? Did they have anything in common? (Compare and Contrast)

En sus brazos tomó mi ensueño
30 y lo arrulló como a un bebé . . .
Y le mató, triste y pequeño,
falto de luz, falto de fe . . .

Juventud, divino tesoro,
¡te fuiste para no volver!
35 Cuando quiero llorar, no lloro,
y a veces lloro sin querer . . .

Otra juzgó que era mi boca
el estuche⁴ de su pasión
y que me **roería,** loca,
40 con sus dientes el corazón

poniendo en un amor de exceso
la mira de su voluntad,
mientras eran abrazo y beso
síntesis de la eternidad:

45 y de nuestra carne ligera
imaginar siempre un Edén,
sin pensar que la Primavera
y la carne acaban también . . .

⁴case

PALABRAS CLAVE
roer   *to gnaw*

Juventud, divino tesoro,
50 ¡ya te vas para no volver!
Cuando quiero llorar, no lloro,
¡y a veces lloro sin querer!

¡Y las demás!, en tantos climas,
en tantas tierras, siempre son,
55 si no **pretexto** de mis rimas,
fantasmas de mi corazón.

En vano busqué a la princesa
que estaba triste de esperar.
La vida es dura. Amarga y pesa.
60 ¡Ya no hay princesa que cantar!

Mas a pesar del tiempo **terco,**
mi sed de amor no tiene fin;
con el cabello gris me acerco
a los rosales del jardín . . .

65 Juventud, divino tesoro,
¡ya te vas para no volver! . . .
Cuando quiero llorar, no lloro,
y a veces lloro sin querer . . .

¡Mas es mía el Alba de oro!

MÁRCALO > **ANÁLISIS**
Rhyme is the repetition of the same sound at the end of two or more lines of poetry, after the last stressed vowel. Read the stanzas in the boxed text and underline the words that rhyme. Use different colors to underline each pair of words.

APUNTES

A pensar...

Does the title of the poem involve sadness or happiness? In general, what are the meanings of fall and spring? What elements of the poem are related to each season? **(Evaluate)**

PALABRAS CLAVE
el pretexto *excuse*   **terco(a)** *obstinate*

Vocabulario de la lectura

Palabras clave

el alba *(fem.)* *dawn*   **la gasa** *gauze*   **el pretexto** *excuse*

el armiño *ermine; soft fur*   **halagador(a)** *flattering*   **roer** *to gnaw*

celeste *celestial*   **el peplo** *peplum, Roman tunic*   **terco(a)** *obstinate*

el duelo *mourning*

A. Completa las oraciones con las **palabras clave** apropiadas. Escribe los verbos en su forma correcta. Luego ordena las letras de las casillas para completar la última oración.

1. El primer amor del autor era tan puro que lo compara con un

   __ __ __ __ __ ☐ .

2. Otra mujer fue más sensible y __ __ __ __ __ __ __ __ __ ☐ .

3. El autor compara la suavidad de ese amor con una túnica de __ __ ☐ __ .

4. Otro amor le dijo que le __ __ ☐ __ ☐ __ el corazón.

5. Darío concluye que sus amores son un ☐ __ __ __ __ __ __ __ para escribir.

   La __ __ __ __ __ __ de Rubén Darío resume sus sentimientos.

B. Completa las siguientes oraciones con la **palabra clave** correcta.

1. La gente que trabaja en el campo se despierta durante el ...

   a. peplo   b. terco   c. alba

2. Diana está muy enferma, pero es muy ... y no quiere ir al doctor.

   a. celeste   b. halagadora   c. terca

3. Los griegos y los romanos se vestían con ... de tela muy fina.

   a. armiños   b. peplos   c. duelos

4. Con un telescopio se pueden observar los cuerpos ...

   a. tercos   b. armiños   c. celestes

5. La familia Linares está de ... pues el tío Leonardo ha muerto.

   a. duelo   b. alba   c. pretexto

¿Comprendiste?

1. ¿El narrador es una persona joven o un hombre mayor? ¿Qué versos lo indican?

_____

_____

2. ¿Qué significan los versos «Plural ha sido la celeste historia de mi corazón»?

_____

3. ¿Por qué el autor compara a su primer amor con Herodías y Salomé?

_____

4. ¿Qué opina el autor sobre las mujeres que ha conocido?

_____

_____

5. ¿Qué mensaje da Rubén Darío cuando dice «¡Mas es mía el Alba de oro!»?

_____

_____

Conexión personal

¿Ha cambiado tu opinión sobre la juventud después de leer el poema? ¿Cómo te sentirías si el tiempo pasara y no encontraras la persona ideal para compartir tu vida? ¿Piensas que hay alguna edad en la que ya hay que dejar de pensar en el amor? Explica.

Creo que durante la juventud...

_____

_____

_____

_____

_____

_____

Para leer   *La muñeca menor*

Reading Strategy

UNDERSTAND CAUSE AND EFFECT Two events are related as cause and effect if one brings about, or causes, the other. The event that happens first is the cause; the one that follows is the effect. Sometimes the first event may cause more than one thing to happen. Complete the following chart with cause-and-effect relationships from "La muñeca menor."

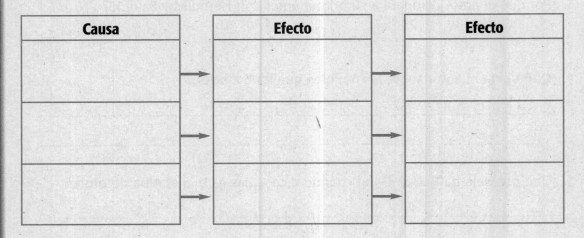

Causa	Efecto	Efecto

What You Need to Know

In Latin American culture, when women get married it is common for them to receive a personal belonging from a close relative as a gift. Usually, the mother, the grandmother, or the aunt of the bride gives her something that she received when she got married or something that she specially made for that occasion. The tradition is based on the hope that passing on those gifts will bring the bride good luck in her marriage and preserve the union of the family. You are about to read the first part of «La muñeca menor» by Rosario Ferré —the story of a family in Puerto Rico that followed this tradition, accompanied by mysterious events.

Sobre la autora

Rosario Ferré nació en Ponce, Puerto Rico, en 1942. Cursó estudios universitarios en su país e hizo un doctorado en la Universidad de Maryland. En Puerto Rico publicó la revista *Zona de carga y descarga* y ha vivido alternativamente entre Washington y San Juan. Sus libros son una mezcla perfecta de lenguaje e imaginación. Además de hablar del mundo interior de las personas también toca el mundo social de su país. Entre su obra narrativa se destacan *Papeles de Pandora*, *La caja de cristal* y *La muñeca menor,* además de numerosas críticas que escribió para publicaciones de ambos países.

READING TIP This short story is very descriptive. Pay attention to all the descriptions written by the author, especially the ones related to the dolls. You may be tempted to skip over the descriptions. If you do, you will miss how important the dolls are to the family.

APUNTES

La muñeca menor

La tía vieja había sacado desde muy temprano el sillón al balcón que daba al **cañaveral** como hacía siempre que se despertaba con ganas de hacer una muñeca.

5 De joven se bañaba a menudo en el río, pero un día en que la lluvia había recrecido la corriente en cola de dragón había sentido en el tuétano[1] de los huesos una mullida sensación de nieve. La cabeza metida en el reverbero[2]

10 negro de las rocas, había creído escuchar, revolcados con el sonido del agua, los estallidos del salitre sobre la playa y pensó que sus cabellos habían llegado por fin a desembocar en el mar. En ese preciso

15 momento sintió una mordida terrible en la **pantorrilla.** La sacaron del agua gritando y se la llevaron a la casa en parihuelas[3] retorciéndose de dolor.

[1] marrow   [2] reflection   [3] stretcher

PALABRAS CLAVE
el cañaveral *canebrake*   **la pantorrilla** *calf*

A pensar...

How could the woman have avoided being bitten by the *chágara*? Why do you think the doctor at first did not realize that the *chágara* was in the woman's leg? Was he negligent in not suspecting that the animal was in her leg? What would happen if the woman decided to remove the animal? Write your answer in the space below. **(Infer)**

APUNTES

El médico que la examinó aseguró que no era
20 nada, probablemente había sido mordida por
una **chágara** viciosa. Sin embargo pasaron los
días y la **llaga** no cerraba. Al cabo de un mes
el médico había llegado a la conclusión de que
la chágara se había introducido dentro de la
25 carne blanda de la pantorrilla, donde había
evidentemente comenzado a engordar. Indicó
que le aplicaran un sinapismo[4] para que el
calor la obligara a salir. La tía estuvo una
semana con la pierna rígida, cubierta de
30 mostaza desde el tobillo hasta el muslo, pero
al finalizar el tratamiento se descubrió que la
llaga se había abultado aún más,
recubriéndose de una substancia pétrea[5] y
limosa que era imposible tratar de remover
35 sin que peligrara toda la pierna. Entonces se
resignó a vivir para siempre con la chágara
enroscada dentro de la gruta de su pantorrilla.

Había sido muy hermosa, pero la chágara que
escondía bajo los largos pliegues de gasa de
40 sus faldas la había despojado de toda vanidad.
Se había encerrado en la casa rehusando a
todos sus pretendientes. Al principio se había
dedicado a la crianza de las hijas de su
hermana, arrastrando por toda la casa la
45 pierna monstruosa con bastante agilidad. Por
aquella época la familia vivía rodeada de un
pasado que dejaba desintegrar a su alrededor

[4] sinapism, a medical plaster made with mustard   [5] rocky, hard

PALABRAS CLAVE
la chágara *river crab*   **limoso(a)** *slimy*
la llaga *sore*

con la misma impasible musicalidad con que
la lámpara de cristal del comedor se
50 desgranaba[6] a pedazos sobre el mantel raído[7]
de la mesa. Las niñas adoraban a la tía. Ella
las peinaba, las bañaba y les daba de comer.
Cuando les leía cuentos se sentaban a su
alrededor y levantaban con disimulo el
55 volante almidonado[8] de su falda para oler el
perfume de **guanábana** madura que
supuraba la pierna en estado de quietud.

Cuando las niñas fueron creciendo la tía se
dedicó a hacerles muñecas para jugar. Al
60 principio eran sólo muñecas comunes, con
carne de guata[9] de higuera[10] y ojos de botones
perdidos. Pero con el pasar del tiempo fue
refinando su arte hasta ganarse el respeto y la
reverencia de toda la familia. El nacimiento de
65 una muñeca era siempre motivo de regocijo
sagrado, lo cual explicaba el que jamás se les
hubiese ocurrido vender una de ellas, ni
siquiera cuando las niñas eran ya grandes y la
familia comenzaba a pasar necesidad. La tía
70 había ido agrandando el tamaño de las
muñecas de manera que correspondieran a la
estatura y a las medidas de cada una de las
niñas. Como eran nueve y la tía hacía una
muñeca de cada niña por año, hubo que
75 separar una pieza de la casa para que la
habitasen exclusivamente las muñecas.

---

[6] it fell apart   [7] worn out   [8] starched   [9] wood shavings
[10] fig tree

PALABRAS CLAVE
la guanábana   *soursop, custard apple*
supurar   *to suppurate, to form or discharge pus*

READER'S SUCCESS STRATEGY The events in the story build to create a sense of suspense. As you read, create an outline including each of those events.

A pensar...

This selection of «La muñeca menor» covers two parts. What are they? Provide details for each one. Which one do you think will be more relevant at the end of the story? (**Identify Main Idea and Details**)

Cuando la mayor cumplió diez y ocho años había ciento veintiséis muñecas de todas las edades en la habitación. Al abrir la puerta,

80 daba la sensación de entrar en un palomar, o en el cuarto de muñecas del palacio de las tzarinas[11], o en un almacén donde alguien había puesto a madurar una larga hilera de hojas de tabaco. Sin embargo, la tía no entraba

85 en la habitación por ninguno de estos placeres, sino que echaba el pestillo[12] a la puerta e iba levantando amorosamente cada una de las muñecas canturreándoles mientras las mecía: Así eras cuando tenías un año, así

90 cuando tenías dos, así cuando tenías tres, reviviendo la vida de cada una de ellas por la dimensión del hueco que le dejaban entre los brazos.

El día que la mayor de las niñas cumplió diez

95 años, la tía se sentó en el sillón frente al cañaveral y no se volvió a levantar jamás. Se balconeaba días enteros observando los cambios de agua de las cañas y sólo salía de su sopor cuando la venía a visitar el doctor o

100 cuando se despertaba con ganas de hacer una muñeca. Comenzaba entonces a clamar para que todos los habitantes de la casa viniesen a ayudarla. Podía verse ese día a los peones de la hacienda haciendo constantes relevos al

105 pueblo como alegres mensajeros incas, a comprar cera, a comprar barro de porcelana, encajes, agujas, carretes de hilos de todos los

MÁRCALO ANÁLISIS A simile is a comparison of one thing with another using the word **como** in Spanish or the words *like or as* in English: for example, *as tall as a tree*. Find and underline the similes in this paragraph.

---

[11] czarinas, Russian empresses   [12] dead bolt

colores. Mientras se llevaban a cabo estas
diligencias, la tía llamaba a su habitación a la
110 niña con la que había soñado esa noche y le
tomaba las medidas. Luego le hacía una
mascarilla de cera que cubría de yeso por
ambos lados como una cara viva dentro de
dos caras muertas; luego hacía salir un hilillo
115 rubio interminable por un hoyito en
la barbilla¹³. La porcelana de las manos era
siempre translúcida; tenía un ligero tinte
marfileño que contrastaba con la blancura
granulada de las caras de biscuit. Para hacer el
120 cuerpo, la tía enviaba al jardín por veinte
higüeras¹⁴ relucientes. Las cogía con una mano
y con un movimiento experto de la cuchilla las
iba **rebanando** una a una en cráneos
relucientes de cuero verde. Luego las inclinaba
125 en hilera contra la pared del balcón, para que
el sol y el aire secaran los cerebros
algodonosos de guano gris. Al cabo de
algunos días raspaba el contenido con una
cuchara y lo iba introduciendo con infinita
130 paciencia por la boca de la muñeca.

Lo único que la tía transigía en utilizar en la
creación de las muñecas sin que estuviese
hecho por ella, eran las bolas de los ojos. Se
los enviaban por correo desde Europa en
135 todos los colores, pero la tía los consideraba
inservibles hasta no haberlos dejado
sumergidos durante un número de días en el
fondo de la quebrada¹⁴ para que aprendiesen

---

¹³ chin   ¹⁴ gourds   ¹⁵ stream

PALABRAS CLAVE
marfileño(a) *like ivory*   **rebanar** *to slice*

A pensar...

Circle the words that give you a
better idea of where the story
takes place and underline the
ones that indicate how much
the aunt is suffering.
(Visualize)

cañaveral	Europa
llaga	miel
muñeca	sopor
nieve	río
supuraba	mar

APUNTES

A pensar...

Next to each sentence, write the numbers 1, 2, 3, 4, 5, or 6 to show the order in which the dolls are made and given away. (Chronological Order)

____ She sinks the eyes in the stream.

____ She observes each niece leaving the house carrying the doll under her arm.

____ She receives the eyes from Europe.

____ She makes the dress.

____ The aunt makes the body from fig trees.

____ She gives a doll to each niece as a wedding gift.

APUNTES

140 a reconocer el más leve movimiento de las antenas de las chágaras. Sólo entonces los lavaba con agua de amoniaco y los guardaba, relucientes como gemas, colocados sobre camas de algodón, en el fondo de una lata de galletas holandesas. El vestido de las muñecas

145 no variaba nunca, a pesar de que las niñas iban creciendo. Vestía siempre a las más pequeñas de tira bordada y a las mayores de broderí[16], colocando en la cabeza de cada una el mismo lazo abullonado[17] y trémulo[18] de

150 pecho de paloma.

Las niñas empezaron a casarse y a abandonar la casa. El día de la boda la tía les regalaba a cada una la última muñeca dándoles un beso en la frente y diciéndoles con una sonrisa:

155 «Aquí tienes tu Pascua de Resurrección.» A los novios los tranquilizaba asegurándoles que la muñeca era sólo una decoración sentimental que solía colocarse sentada, en las casas de antes, sobre la cola del piano. Desde lo alto del

160 balcón la tía observaba a las niñas bajar por última vez las escaleras de la casa sosteniendo en una mano la modesta maleta a cuadros de cartón y pasando el otro brazo alrededor de la cintura de aquella exuberante muñeca hecha a

165 su imagen y semejanza, calzada con zapatillas de ante[19], faldas de bordados nevados y **pantaletas** de valenciennes. Las manos y la cara de estas muñecas, sin embargo, se

---

[16] embroidered cotton fabric   [17] airy, gauzy   [18] shaking
[19] elk

PALABRAS CLAVE
  la pantaleta   *pantalet, long underpants extending below the skirt*

notaban menos transparentes, tenían la
170 consistencia de la leche cortada. Esta
diferencia encubría otra más sutil: la muñeca
de boda no estaba jamás rellena de guata, sino
de miel.

Ya se habían casado todas las niñas y en la
175 casa quedaba sólo la más joven cuando el
doctor hizo a la tía la visita mensual
acompañado de su hijo que acababa de
regresar de sus estudios de medicina en el
norte. El joven levantó el volante de la falda
180 almidonada y se quedó mirando aquella
inmensa vejiga abotagada [20] que manaba una
esperma [21] perfumada por la punta de sus
escamas verdes. Sacó su estetoscopio y la
auscultó cuidadosamente. La tía pensó que
185 auscultaba la respiración de la chágara para
verificar si todavía estaba viva, y cogiéndole
la mano con cariño se la puso sobre un lugar
determinado para que palpara [22] el
movimiento constante de las antenas. El joven
190 dejó caer la falda y miró fijamente al padre.
Usted hubiese podido haber curado esto en
sus comienzos, le dijo. Es cierto, contestó el
padre, pero yo sólo quería que vinieras a ver
la chágara que te había pagado los estudios
195 durante veinte años.

[20] inflamed   [21] thick fluid   [22] so that he would feel

||| MÁRCALO > ANÁLISIS

The **protagonist** is the main
character in a story or play
—the one around which the
main action occurs. In the
boxed text you will read about
several characters. Circle the
one you think is the protagonist
of this story and explain why
on the lines below.

_____

_____

_____

CHALLENGE In the last
paragraph of the selection,
another character shows up
—the doctor's son. What do you
think his intentions will be after
discovering that his father
could have cured the woman?
Pay attention to the characters
in that scene and to the
dialogue between father and
son. How do you think the
story might end? **(Predict)**

_____

_____

_____

_____

_____

_____

_____

Vocabulario de la lectura

Palabras clave

el cañaveral *canebrake*

la chágara *river crab*

la guanábana *soursop, custard apple*

limoso(a) *slimy*

la llaga *sore*

marfileño(a) *like ivory*

la pantaleta *pantalet, long underpants extending below the skirt*

la pantorrilla *calf*

rebanar *to slice*

supurar *to suppurate, to form or discharge pus*

A. Completa cada analogía con una **palabra clave**. En una analogía, las últimas dos palabras deben estar relacionadas de la misma manera que los primeras dos.

1. NOCHE : DÍA : : seco : _____

2. BRAZO : CODO :: pierna : _____

3. LECHUGA : ESPINACA :: _____ : piña

4. UNIR : SEPARAR :: JUNTAR :: _____

5. CALCETÍN : PIE :: _____ :: PIERNA

B. Escribe un párrafo breve para resumir lo que ocurre en «La muñeca menor», usando todas las **palabras clave** que puedas.

_____

_____

_____

_____

_____

_____

_____

_____

¿Comprendiste?

1. ¿Qué le ocurrió a la tía? ¿En dónde le ocurrió eso?

_____

2. ¿Con quién vivía la tía y cómo reaccionaban estas personas frente al problema de su tía?

_____

3. ¿Cuándo dejaba de darles muñecas a sus sobrinas?

_____

4. ¿Qué tipo de mentira le dijo el médico?

_____

5. ¿Por qué crees que el cuento se llama «La muñeca menor»?

_____

Conexión personal

¿Alguna vez has sido mordido(a) o atacado por algún animal salvaje? ¿Conoces a alguien a quien le haya ocurrido algo parecido? ¿Has visto alguna película sobre el tema? En el espacio de abajo explica lo que ocurrió, de qué animal se trataba, dónde pasó, qué hubo que hacer y cuáles fueron las consecuencias.

El animal que atacó era...

_____

_____

_____

_____

_____

_____

_____

_____

_____

Para leer   *Borges y yo / Arte poética*

Reading Strategy

CATEGORIZE DESCRIPTIONS Some works contain vivid descriptions, or details that help readers form strong mental pictures. These images may be of characters, settings, or events, and they always appeal to one or more of the five senses. Borges uses descriptions that allow the reader to understand his feelings. Fill in the chart below with details from Borges' selections and identify the senses *(vista, oído, gusto, tacto u olfato)* they appeal to.

Descripción	Sentido

What You Need to Know

People often ask themselves two questions. One is related to identity; their actions are not always reflected by the way they think and feel. Many times, their achievements are of a material nature, although internally they wish for other things. It may seem that they are made of two parts: the things they do and the things they wish for. The other question is related to where they come from and where they are going. Through works like «Borges y yo» and «Arte poética,» Jorge Luis Borges has posed these and other questions related to identity and time.

Sobre el autor

Jorge Luis Borges (1899–1986) nació en Buenos Aires, Argentina. En 1914 viajó a Europa con su familia y se instaló en Ginebra (Suiza) donde cursó el bachillerato para luego mudarse a España. Al regresar a Buenos Aires, fundó la revista *Proa.* En 1944 publicó *Ficciones,* un libro de cuentos por el cual obtuvo el Gran Premio de la Sociedad Argentina de Escritores. Más tarde fue nombrado director de la Biblioteca Nacional. Su amor por la literatura inglesa lo llevó a ser profesor de la Universidad de Buenos Aires. Su lenguaje literario fue cambiando hasta tratar temas de metafísica, dándole una creciente importancia a la psicología de sus personajes. Ha recibido numerosos premios literarios en todo el mundo, incluido el Premio Cervantes.

Borges y yo

Al otro, a Borges, es a quien le ocurren las cosas. Yo camino por Buenos Aires y me demoro[1], acaso ya mecánicamente, para mirar el arco de un zaguán[2] y la puerta cancel[3]; de
5 Borges tengo noticias por el correo y veo su nombre en una **terna** de profesores o en un diccionario biográfico. Me gustan los relojes de arena, los mapas, la tipografía del siglo XVIII, las etimologías, el sabor del café y la
10 prosa de Stevenson[4]; el otro comparte esas preferencias, pero de un modo vanidoso que las convierte en atributos de un actor. Sería exagerado afirmar que nuestra relación es hostil; yo vivo, yo me dejo vivir, para que
15 Borges pueda **tramar** su literatura y esa literatura me justifica.

---

[1] I stop   [2] doorway   [3] inner door to keep out airdrafts
[4] British writer from nineteenth century

PALABRAS CLAVE
la terna   *list of three candidates*   **tramar**   *to plan a difficult project*

READING TIP «Borges y yo» is a self-analysis by the author. As you read, look for evidence of the author's character traits to know what type of person he is.

APUNTES

MÁRCALO ANÁLISIS A **catalog** is a list of people, things, or attributes in a narration or poem. Read the boxed text and underline the catalog.

APUNTES

LITERATURA
ADICIONAL

APUNTES

Nada me cuesta confesar que ha logrado
ciertas páginas válidas, pero esas páginas no
me pueden salvar, quizá porque lo bueno ya
no es de nadie, ni siquiera del otro, sino del
lenguaje o la tradición. Por lo demás, yo estoy
destinado a perderme, definitivamente, y sólo
algún instante de mí podrá sobrevivir en el
otro. Poco a poco voy cediéndole todo,
aunque me consta su perversa costumbre de
falsear y magnificar. Spinoza[5] entendió que
todas las cosas quieren perseverar en su ser; la
piedra eternamente quiere ser piedra y el tigre
un tigre. Yo he de quedar en Borges, no en mí
(si es que alguien soy), pero me reconozco
menos en sus libros que en muchos otros o
que en el laborioso rasgueo[6] de una guitarra.
Hace años yo traté de librarme de él y pasé de
las mitologías del **arrabal** a los juegos con el
tiempo y con lo infinito, pero esos juegos son
de Borges ahora y tendré que **idear** otras
cosas. Así mi vida es una fuga[7] y todo lo
pierdo y todo es del olvido, o del otro.

No sé cuál de los dos escribe esta página.

[5] Dutch philosopher   [6] strumming   [7] escape

A pensar...

Match the sentences in the first column with the words of the second column that define the characteristics of Borges. (Evaluate)

Al otro es a quien se le ocurren las cosas.	recognition
Veo su nombre en una terna.	confusion
Traté de librarme de las mitologías del arrabal.	humbleness
No sé cuál de los dos escribe esta página.	style change

PALABRAS CLAVE
el arrabal *suburb*   **idear** *to think up, to invent*

Arte poética

Mirar el río hecho de tiempo y agua
Y recordar que el tiempo es otro río,
Saber que nos perdemos como el río
Y que los rostros pasan como el agua.

5 Sentir que la **vigilia** es otro sueño
Que sueña no soñar y que la muerte
Que teme nuestra carne es esa muerte
De cada noche, que se llama sueño.

Ver en el día o en el año un símbolo
10 De los días del hombre y de sus años,
Convertir el ultraje¹ de los años
En una música, un rumor y un símbolo,

Ver en la muerte el sueño, en el **ocaso**
Un triste oro, tal es la poesía
15 Que es inmortal y pobre. La poesía
Vuelve como la **aurora** y el ocaso.

A veces en las tardes una cara
Nos mira desde el fondo de un espejo;
El arte debe ser como ese espejo
20 Que nos revela nuestra propia cara.

¹outrage

READER'S SUCCESS STRATEGY To establish his thinking about identity and time, Borges uses complex descriptions. As you read each section of the selections, try to restate difficult sentences in your own words. Look for context clues to help you figure out meaning.

READING TIP «Arte poética» refers to the author's point of view about eternity. Pay attention to the elements that he compares with time.

A pensar...

In the poem, Borges includes several comparisons that might sound contradictory. Choose one and explain what you think the author means. **(Analyze)**

PALABRAS CLAVE
la vigilia *sleeplesness*
el ocaso *sunset*
la aurora *dawn*

CHALLENGE Can you make any connection between «Borges y yo» and «Arte poética»? What elements of time and identity appear in both readings? Does the author express the same kinds of feelings in both works? Explain your ideas on the lines below. **(Connect)**

Cuentan que Ulises[2], harto de prodigios,
Lloró de amor al **divisar** su Itaca[3]
Verde y humilde. El arte es esa Itaca
De verde eternidad, no de prodigios.

25   También es como el río interminable
Que pasa y queda y es cristal de un mismo
Heráclito[4] inconstante, que es el mismo
Y es otro, como el río interminable.

[2]Greek hero, king of Ithaca   [3]Greek island
[4]Greek philosopher who stated that strife and change
  are the natural conditions of the universe.

PALABRAS CLAVE
divisar   *to discern*

Vocabulario de la lectura

Palabras clave

el arrabal *suburb*

la aurora *dawn*

divisar *to discern*

idear *to think up, to invent*

el ocaso *sunset*

la terna *list of three candidates*

tramar *to plan a difficult project*

la vigilia *sleeplesnes*

A. En la línea que aparece al lado de cada par de palabras, escribe si éstas son **sinónimos** o **antónimos**. Recuerda que los sinónimos son palabras que tienen el mismo significado mientras que los antónimos tienen significados opuestos.

1. divisar - perder _____

2. vigilia - sueño _____

3. alba - ocaso _____

4. tramar - pensar _____

5. aurora - amanecer _____

B. Para explicar la relación entre los dos Borges de «Borges y yo», haz un círculo alrededor de la **palabra clave** que mejor complete cada oración.

1. Uno de los Borges aparece en una (terna / vigilia) de profesores.

2. El Borges que narra, en sus comienzos escribía sobre el (arrabal / ocaso).

3. Borges menciona a Ulises (divisando / tramando) su Itaca.

4. Un Borges deja que el otro (trame / idee) su literatura.

5. Borges, el narrador, ya no quiere escribir sobre el infinito. Él quiere (divisar / idear) otras cosas.

¿Comprendiste?

1. «Borges y yo» trata de dos identidades. ¿Cuál de las dos está narrando la historia?

_____

2. ¿Borges cosidera que su trabajo literario ha tenido valor? ¿Cómo lo expresa?

_____

3. ¿Qué temas desarrolló el autor durante sus obras y cuáles son sus planes para el futuro?

_____

4. En «Arte poética», ¿qué significa el verso «el arte debe ser como ese espejo»?

_____

5. ¿Qué significa la comparación con Ulises?

_____

Conexión personal

¿Alguna vez has sufrido un conflicto de identidad? ¿Has pensado que lo que haces no siempre coincide con lo que sientes? Escribe tus experiencias en el espacio de abajo. Además de tus sentimientos, también puedes incluir lugares en los que has vivido, con los que no te hayas sentido identificado(a). Si no has sufrido esos conflictos, explica cuál es el motivo de tu seguridad.

Yo experimenté lo siguiente:

_____

_____

_____

_____

_____

_____

_____

_____

_____

_____

_____

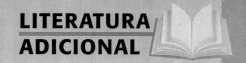

Para leer   *Romance sonámbulo*

Reading Strategy

INDICATE SOUND DEVICES Poets use **sound devices** such as
repetition, rhyme, and rhythm to create mood and to convey
meaning. **Rhythm,** one of the most common poetic sound devices,
is a pattern of stressed and unstressed syllables. When the poem
is read aloud, the rhythm can be heard in the greater emphasis
on the same syllables than on the others. Choose four lines
from "Romance sonámbulo" and write them in the chart below.
Indicate the rhythmical pattern that you hear by marking the
stressed (´) and unstressed (˘) syllables.

Romance sonámbulo

_____

_____

_____

_____

What You Need to Know

Romances are poems of Spanish origin in which the even verses have the
same rhyme and, in general, each line has eight syllables. There are also
romances in prose, whose main themes are generally a poetic point of
view of a historical event. *Romances* were very popular in the the
fifteenth century, since people could sing them while playing a musical
instrument, dancing, or attending an informal gathering. In 1928, García
Lorca wrote *Romancero gitano*, a collection of *romances* that combine
both poetry and historical events. Also, some of García Lorca's *romances*,
like «Romance sonámbulo,» became very popular songs.

READING TIP This poem alternates the voice of the poet with the dialogue between the characters. Pay attention to the punctuation marks so that you can realize who is talking.

APUNTES

Sobre el autor

Federico García Lorca (1898-1936) nació en Fuente Vaqueros, en la provincia de Granada, España. En 1929 viajó a Estados Unidos, donde escribió *Poeta en Nueva York.* Como dramaturgo revolucionó el mundo del teatro. Sus obras se basan principalmente en situaciones dramáticas, usando un lenguaje muy atrevido para su época. En poesía se destacó con *Romancero gitano,* una colección de poemas que hablan del amor y de la política en España. Al estallar la Guerra Civil Española, fue fusilado por el ejército del general Franco.

Romance sonámbulo

A Gloria Giner y
A Fernando de los Ríos

Verde que te quiero verde.
Verde viento. Verdes ramas.
El barco sobre la mar
y el caballo en la montaña.
5 Con la sombra en la cintura,
ella sueña en su **baranda,**
verde carne, pelo verde,
con ojos de fría plata.
Verde que te quiero verde.
10 Bajo la luna gitana,
las cosas la están mirando
y ella no puede mirarlas.

PALABRAS CLAVE
la baranda *railing*

Verde que te quiero verde.
Grandes estrellas de escarcha [1]
15 vienen con el pez de sombra
que abre el camino del alba.
La higuera frota su viento
con la lija [2] de sus ramas,
y el monte, gato garduño [3],
20 eriza [4] sus pitas [5] agrias.
Pero ¿quién vendrá? ¿Y por dónde?…
Ella sigue en su baranda,
verde carne, pelo verde,
soñando en la mar amarga.

25   —**Compadre,** quiero cambiar
mi caballo por su casa,
mi **montura** por su espejo,
mi cuchillo por su manta.
Compadre, vengo sangrando,
30 desde los puertos de Cabra [6].
—Si yo pudiera, **mocito,**
este trato se cerraba.
Pero yo ya no soy yo,
ni mi casa es ya mi casa.
35 —Compadre, quiero morir
decentemente en mi cama.
De acero, si puede ser,
con las sábanas de holanda [7].
¿No ves la herida que tengo
40 desde el pecho a la garganta?

---

[1] frost   [2] sandpaper   [3] thief   [4] it stiffens
[5] green plants with spiny leaves   [6] town in Spain
[7] fine cotton fabric, originating from Holland

PALABRAS CLAVE
   el compadre   *intimate friend*   **el mocito**   *young man*
   la montura   *saddle*   **decentemente**   *decently, honorably*

READER'S
SUCCESS
STRATEGY   To better understand
how many people are
involved in this poem,
highlight the words that
represent each person on
these pages:

A pensar…

Make a list of the events in this
part of the poem. Consider who
is coming, whom that person is
looking for, who meets that
person, and how they feel.
(Summarize)

LITERATURA ADICIONAL

▥ MÁRCALO ⧓ **ANÁLISIS**

Alliteration is the repetition of the same vowel or consonant sounds at the beginning of words in a line of poetry, to give the poem a musical sense. Read the boxed text and underline the example of alliteration.

A pensar...

Try to picture the scene where the poem occurs. Based on the images described by García Lorca, say what the building the two men are going into is like, what time of day it is, and what the weather is like. **(Visualize)**

_____

_____

_____

_____

_____

_____

_____

_____

_____

_____

_____

_____

_____

_____

—Trescientas rosas morenas
lleva tu **pechera** blanca.
Tu sangre **rezuma** y huele
alrededor de tu faja.
45 Pero yo ya no soy yo,
ni mi casa es ya mi casa.
—Dejadme subir al menos
hasta las altas barandas,
¡dejadme subir!, dejadme
50 hasta las verdes barandas.
Barandales de la luna
por donde retumba[8] el agua.

Ya suben los dos compadres
hacia las altas barandas.
55 Dejando un rastro de sangre.
Dejando un rastro de lágrimas.
Temblaban en los tejados
farolillos de hojalata[9].
Mil panderos[10] de cristal
60 herían la madrugada.

_____

[8] it rumbles   [9] tinplate   [10] large tambourines

PALABRAS CLAVE
la pechera _shirt front_   **rezumar** _to exude, to leak_

Verde que te quiero verde,
verde viento, verdes ramas.
Los dos compadres subieron.
El largo viento dejaba
65 en la boca un raro gusto
de hiel[11], de menta y de albahaca[12].
—¡Compadre! ¿Dónde está, dime,
dónde está tu niña amarga?
—¡Cuántas veces te esperó,
70 ¡Cuántas veces te esperara,
cara fresca, negro pelo,
en esta verde baranda!

Sobre el rostro del **aljibe**
se mecía la gitana.
75 Verde carne, pelo verde,
con ojos de fría plata.
Un carámbano[13] de luna
la sostiene sobre el agua.
La noche se puso íntima
80 como una pequeña plaza.
Guardias civiles[14] borrachos
en la puerta golpeaban.
Verde que te quiero verde.
Verde viento. Verdes ramas.
85 El barco sobre la mar
Y el caballo en la montaña.

---

[11] centaury, perennial plant; bile   [12] basil   [13] icicle
[14] Spanish troops in charge of keeping order

PALABRAS CLAVE
el aljibe *well, cistern*

Vocabulario de la lectura

Palabras clave

el **aljibe**   *well, cistern*

la **baranda**   *railing*

el **compadre**   *intimate friend*

decentemente   *decently, honorably*

el **mocito**   *young man*

la **montura**   *saddle*

la **pechera**   *shirt front*

rezumar   *to exude, to leak*

A. Empareja cada **palabra clave** con la definición correcta. En la línea que figura al lado de cada palabra, escribe la letra correspondiente a la definición de dicha palabra.

_____ 1. decentemente

_____ 2. rezumar

_____ 3. mocito

_____ 4. montura

_____ 5. aljibe

A. joven

B. silla para montar a caballo

C. con honra; como debe ser

D. pozo de donde se saca agua

E. que sale del cuerpo

B. Completa los espacios en blanco con la **palabra clave** correcta.

En «Romance sonámbulo», la muchacha esperó a su enamorado por mucho

tiempo en su _____. Cuando el enamorado llegó, éste tenía
(1)

manchas de sangre en su _____. Le dijo a su _____ que
(2)   (3)

quería ver a la muchacha y le ofreció su _____ a cambio. La
(4)

muchacha ya no estaba pero su cara se reflejaba en el _____.
(5)

¿Comprendiste?

1. La palabra **sonámbulo** significa *sleepwalking*. ¿Cómo se relaciona esta palabra con el tema del poema?

   _____

2. ¿Cómo es el lugar que atraviesa el joven antes de llegar al pueblo?

   _____

3. ¿En qué condiciones llega el joven al pueblo?

   _____

4. ¿Qué elementos en común tienen las palabras **hiel, menta** y **albahaca**?

   _____

5. ¿Qué significado crees que tiene la palabra **verde** en el poema?

   _____

Conexión personal

Piensa en algún momento de tu vida en que hayas ido en busca de algo o de alguien y no lo encontraste. ¿Qué buscabas? ¿Qué obstáculos tuviste que pasar para llegar? ¿Cuál fue el resultado y a qué conclusión llegaste? Puedes referirte a personas, objetos o logros personales.

Yo buscaba...

_____

_____

_____

_____

_____

_____

_____

_____

Para leer   *Un cuentecillo triste*

Reading Strategy

ANALYZE TEXT STRUCTURE Writers of fiction present details about the characters and the setting and organize the information in various ways. Writers may use comparison and contrast, chronological order, or spatial order. When you analyze text structure, look for one of these patterns. Practice analyzing text structure by reading the first two pages of "Un cuentecillo triste." Then answer the questions in the chart below.

Un cuentecillo triste	
¿En cuántas partes dividirías esta sección?	
¿Qué oración indica el comienzo de cada parte?	
¿Cuál es la idea principal de cada parte?	
Escribe algunas palabras del cuento que indiquen la idea general.	

What You Need to Know

Personal advertisements in newspapers and magazines are very popular all over the world, and Latin America is no exception. Many of these ads help people that are alone or shy to meet somebody and start a relationship. Some of the personal ads are placed individually by each person, but in general they are managed by professional agencies. The agencies file a record of each person, including his or her resume, qualities, personal interests, and photographs. In many cases, these meetings end in good friendships and sometimes people even get married. But very often, people get disenchanted because they don't see the results they were expecting. In «Un cuentecillo triste» Gabriel García Márquez narrates the story of such a meeting.

Sobre el autor

Gabriel García Márquez nació en Aracataca, Colombia en 1928. Es uno de los exponentes del realismo mágico, por lo que en sus obras habla de la realidad colombiana dándole un toque fantástico. La política casi siempre está presente en sus trabajos, y muchas veces ha tenido problemas de censura. Trabajó como periodista y tuvo su propia columna en el periódico *El Heraldo*, donde publicó artículos y cuentos cortos, como «Un cuentecillo triste». Sus obras han ganado prestigio internacional; entre ellas figuran *Cien años de soledad*, *Relato de un náufrago* y *El amor en los tiempos del cólera*. García Márquez formó parte del «boom» de escritores latinoamericanos que estalló en la década de 1960. En el año 1982 recibió el Premio Nóbel de Literatura.

Un cuentecillo triste

Se aburría de tal modo los domingos en la tarde, que resolvió conseguir una novia. Fue al periódico e insertó un aviso en la sección de clasificados: «Joven de 23 años, 1.72, cuyo[1]
5 único defecto es aburrirse los domingos en la tarde, desea probar relaciones con una muchacha de su misma edad».

Aguardó tres días. Uno de ellos, domingo, estuvo al borde del suicidio, parado tres horas
10 en una esquina, viendo el pasar de las gentes. Pero el martes recibió una carta. Era una muchacha que decía ser amable y comprensiva y que consideraba ser la mujer ideal para un hombre como él, porque ella
15 también se aburría los domingos en la tarde. Le pareció que aquélla era la mujer apropiada.

[1] whose

READING TIP This selection is short but has many details. Try to picture the characters and the setting in your mind. Pay attention to the short dialogues and the reactions of each character.

APUNTES

A pensar...

Why does the man place the ad? Why do you think he does not have another alternative to get what he wants? **(Draw Conclusions)**

READER'S SUCCESS STRATEGY Apparently, there is a communication problem between the characters. To help understand the situation, highlight the phrases and sentences in quotation marks and read them aloud.

APUNTES

_____

_____

_____

_____

_____

_____

_____

_____

_____

_____

_____

▌▌▌ MÁRCALO ▷ ANÁLISIS
Onomatopoeia is the formation of a word by imitating the natural sound associated with the object or action involved. Read the boxed text and highlight the onomatopoeia. Explain what it means.

_____

_____

_____

Le contestó. Ella volvió a escribirle el viernes y le envió un retrato. No era bonita, pero tenía **facciones** agradables y jóvenes. Él le mandó,
20 a su vez, un retrato suyo. Y el viernes, cuando ya el domingo se aproximaba como un fantasma largamente **temido,** se pusieron de acuerdo para encontrarse el domingo a la una de la tarde en un establecimiento de la ciudad.

25 Él llegó a la una en punto con su mejor vestido, bien peinado y con una revista que compró el sábado. Ella estaba esperándolo, visiblemente emocionada, en una de las mesas del fondo. La reconoció por el retrato y por la
30 **ansiedad** con que miraba hacia la puerta de entrada.

—Hola —dijo él.

Ella sonrió. Le tendió la mano, le dijo un musical: «Qué hubo», mientras él se sentaba a
35 su lado. Él pidió una limonada. Ella dijo que prefería seguir con el helado. Mientras el mozo² traía el **pedido,** él le dijo: «¿Tenías mucho tiempo de estar aquí?» Y ella dijo: «No mucho. Cinco minutos a lo sumo³». Él sonrió
40 comprensivamente, en el instante en que llegaba el mozo con la limonada. Empezó a tomarla con lentitud, mirándola mientras lo hacía. Ella volvió a sonreír. Hizo: «Ji, ji, ji». Y a él le pareció una manera muy curiosa de reírse.

²waiter   ³at the most

PALABRAS CLAVE
las facciones _features (of face)_   **la ansiedad** _anxiety_
temido(a) _feared_   **el pedido** _order_

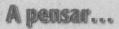

45 «Te traje esta revista», dijo. Ella la tomó en sus manos, la hojeó. Siguió hojeándola **displicentemente** hasta cuando él acabó de comerse el huevo, en medio de un profundo silencio sin salida, eterno, definitivo, que sólo

50 se rompió cuando él miró el reloj de pared y dijo: «Qué barbaridad[4]. Ya van a ser las dos». Y le preguntó: «¿Salimos?» Y ella dijo que sí.

En la calle, después de haber caminado en silencio varias cuadras[5], ella le preguntó:

55 «¿Siempre te aburres los domingos?» Él dijo que sí y ella dijo: «Qué casualidad, yo también». Él sonrió. Dijo: «Bueno, siquiera hoy está haciendo un hermoso día». Ella volvió a reírse con su curioso: «ji, ji, ji» y dijo

60 finalmente: «Es que ya viene diciembre».

A las tres y media, antes de que hubieran hablado más de veinte palabras, pasaron frente a un teatro y él dijo: «¿Entramos?» Y ella dijo: «Bueno». Entraron. Ella lo esperó

65 mientras el portero[6] le entregaba las **contraseñas.** Le dijo: «¿Te gustan los asientos de atrás?» Él dijo que sí. Y como la película era dramática, él apoyó las rodillas en el asiento delantero[7] y se quedó dormido. Ella

70 estuvo despierta diez o quince minutos más. Pero al fin, después de **bostezar** diez veces, se **acurrucó** en la **butaca** y se quedó dormida.

---

[4]My goodness!   [5]blocks   [6]Colombian word for ticket taker
[7]in front (of him)

PALABRAS CLAVE

displicentemente *indifferently*	**acurrucarse** *to get cozy and*
la contraseña *readmission ticket*	*comfortable*
bostezar *to yawn*	**la butaca** *seat*

A pensar...

How do the two characters introduce themselves? What is the relevance of the day that they mention? **(Evaluate)**

CHALLENGE Why do you think the couple fell asleep in the movie theater? Do you believe they had other expectations of each other? If the story continued, what kind of excuses do you think they would give? Is there any chance that they can make this relationship work? Why? **(Predict)**

Vocabulario de la lectura

Palabras clave

acurrucarse *to get cozy and comfortable*

la ansiedad *anxiety*

bostezar *to yawn*

la butaca *theater seats*

la contraseña *readmission ticket*

displicentemente *indifferently*

facciones *features (of face)*

el pedido *order*

temido(a) *feared*

A. Completa el crucigrama con las **palabras clave** correctas.

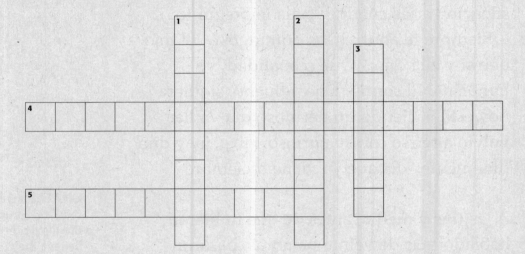

Horizontales

4. Virginia me habló... sin interés.

5. Julián salió del cine a comprar palomitas. Tuvo que mostrar su...

Verticales

1. Teresa sufre de ... ; siempre está apurada por todo.

2. Rodolfo tenía tanto sueño que empezó a ...

3. Finalmente, Marisa se decidió a tomar ese examen tan ...

B. Las siguientes oraciones están relacionadas con «Un cuentecillo triste». Completa cada una con la **palabra clave** correcta. Escribe los verbos en su forma correcta.

1. El joven vio una foto de la muchacha y pensó que tenía _____ agradables.

2. El día del encuentro, la muchacha lo estaba esperando con mucha _____.

3. El mozo trajo el _____: una limonada para el joven.

4. Luego fueron al cine. Él apoyó sus piernas en la _____ de adelante.

5. Un rato después, ella se _____ y se durmió.

¿Comprendiste?

1. ¿Qué tipo de persona es el joven?

_____

2. ¿Cuál fue su reacción al recibir la fotografía de la muchacha?

_____

3. Para que el encuentro hubiera sido más agradable, ¿qué debería haber contestado ella cuando él le preguntó si siempre se aburría los domingos?

_____

4. ¿La idea de ir a ver una película fue buena o había mejores alternativas? Explica.

_____

_____

5. ¿Definirías el final del cuento como trágico o simplemente triste? ¿Es un final previsible (*foreseeable*) o sorpresa? ¿Por qué?

_____

_____

Conexión personal

¿Alguna vez te has citado con alguien por medio del periódico o por anuncios en la radio? ¿Conoces a alguien que lo haya hecho? ¿Crees que este tipo de encuentros puede tener consecuencias positivas o generalmente fallan? Explica tu opinión en el espacio de abajo.

Los encuentros por medio de avisos...

_____

_____

_____

_____

_____

_____

Academic and Informational Reading

In this section you'll find strategies to help you read all kinds of informational materials. The examples here range from magazines you read for fun to textbooks to bus schedules. Applying these simple and effective techniques will help you be a successful reader of the many texts you encounter every day.

Reading a Magazine Article

A magazine article is designed to catch and hold your interest. Learning how to recognize the items on a magazine page will help you read even the most complicated articles. Look at the sample magazine article as you read each strategy below.

A Read the **title** and other **headings** to see what the article is about. The title often presents the main topic of the article.

B Study **visuals**, such as pictures, maps, and photographs. These elements add interest and information to the article.

C Notice any **quotations.** Who is quoted? Evaluate whether the person a reliable source on the subject.

D Think about the author's **explanations** as you read. These often include comparisons that help readers understand new concepts.

E Pay attention to **special features,** such as bulleted lists, charts, tables, and graphs. These provide detailed information on the topic.

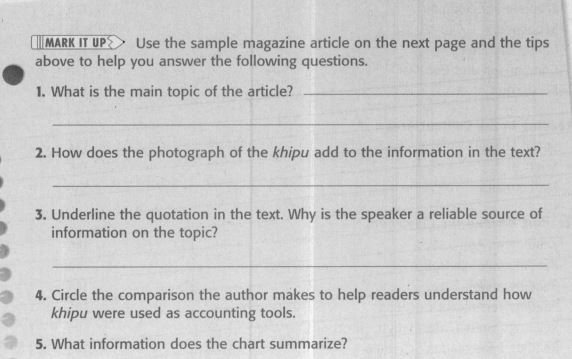

MARK IT UP Use the sample magazine article on the next page and the tips above to help you answer the following questions.

1. What is the main topic of the article? _____

_____

2. How does the photograph of the *khipu* add to the information in the text?

_____

3. Underline the quotation in the text. Why is the speaker a reliable source of information on the topic?

_____

4. Circle the comparison the author makes to help readers understand how *khipu* were used as accounting tools.

5. What information does the chart summarize?

_____

A Untying the Knots:
New Theory of Incan Writing

At the height of their reign—from the mid-15th to the mid-16th centuries—the Inca controlled the entire western coast of South America. They created advanced economic and governmental systems, extensive roads and irrigation networks, and magnificent stone monuments. But, as far as anthropologists knew, the Inca had no system of writing. A recent discovery challenges that long-held assumption.

Professor Gary Urton of Harvard University believes he has discovered not only that the Inca had a writing system, but that it is totally unique. This system, he says, consisted of knotted strings hung on moplike structures called *khipu*. Scholars have known about *khipu* for years, but believed they served as accounting tools—sort of like a fiber abacus. They were thought to be a method of keeping track of numbers, not a way of recording words.

Dr. Urton turned this interpretation around. Ten years of research have led him to believe that the knotted strings were an early form of writing. Meaning was encoded in the way the knots were tied and the pattern in which they were arranged.

E Unique Traits of Incan Knot Writing

Incan Knot Writing	Other Writing Systems
three-dimensional—knots tied in string hung on a frame	two-dimensional—symbols recorded on clay, stone, or paper
binary—two symbols (knot or no knot), like a computer code	multiform—alphabets consisting of many symbols or letters
coded in sequences of seven symbols	coded in varying sequences of symbols or letters

In support of Dr. Urton's interpretation, Dr. Heather Lechtman, an archaeologist at M.I.T., said, "It doesn't surprise me that people would have thought of using *khipu* perhaps for some sort of writing system." Dr. Urton plans to input the sequences of knots he has analyzed into a computer to help people break the Incan writing code—and possibly rewrite history.

Reading a Textbook

The first page of a textbook lesson introduces you to a particular topic. The page also provides important information that will guide you through the rest of the lesson. Look at the sample textbook page as you read each strategy below.

A Preview the **title** and other **headings** to determine the lesson's main topic and related subtopics.

B Read the main **idea, objective,** or **focus.** These items summarize the lesson and help set a purpose for your reading.

C Look for a list of terms or **vocabulary words** at the start of each lesson. These words will be identified and defined throughout the lesson.

D Find words set in special type, such as **italics** and **boldface.** Look for definitions before or after these terms.

E Notice any **special features,** such as extended text enclosed in a tinted box. These may include **direct quotations** from a **primary source** that provided firsthand information or perspective on a topic.

F Examine **visuals,** such as photographs and illustrations, and read their **captions.** Visuals add information and interest to the topic.

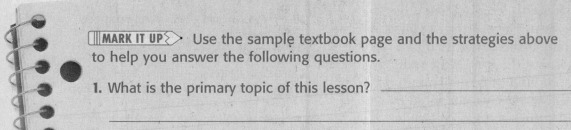

MARK IT UP Use the sample textbook page and the strategies above to help you answer the following questions.

1. What is the primary topic of this lesson? _____

_____

2. Circle the vocabulary terms.

3. Draw a box around the main idea of the lesson.

4. What firsthand information does the quotation in the tint box provide?

_____

5. What is unique about the painting of Christopher Columbus?

_____

(A) **(1)**

Spanish Conquests in the Americas

(C) TERMS & NAMES
• Christopher Columbus
• colony
• Hernando Cortés
• conquistadors
• Montezuma II
• Francisco Pizarro
• mestizo
• *encomienda*

(B) **MAIN IDEA**

The voyages of Columbus prompted the Spanish to carve out the first European colonies in the Americas.

WHY IT MATTERS NOW

Throughout the Americas, Spanish culture, language, and descendants are the legacy of this period.

(D) **SETTING THE STAGE** As you read in the previous chapter, competition for wealth in the East among European nations was fierce. This competition prompted sea captain **Christopher Columbus** to make a daring voyage for Spain in 1492. Instead of sailing east, Columbus sailed west across the Atlantic in search of an alternate trade route to Asia and its riches. Columbus never reached Asia. Instead he stepped onto an island in the Caribbean. That event set in motion a process that would bring together the peoples of Europe, Africa, and the Americas. And the world would change forever.

Columbus's Voyage Paves the Way

No one paid much attention as the *Niña, Pinta,* and *Santa María* slid out of a Spanish port around dawn on August 3, 1492. In a matter of months, however, Columbus's fleet would make history. It would reach the shores of what was to Europeans an astonishing new world.

First Encounters In the early hours of October 12, 1492, the long-awaited cry came. A lookout aboard the *Pinta* caught sight of a shoreline in the distance. *"Tierra! Tierra!"* he shouted. "Land! Land!" By dawn, Columbus and his crew were ashore. Thinking he had successfully reached the East Indies, Columbus called the surprised inhabitants who greeted him, *los indios.* The term translated into "Indian," a word mistakenly applied to all the native peoples of the Americas. In his memoirs, Columbus recounted his first meeting with the native peoples:

THINK THROUGH HISTORY
A. Clarifying
Why did Columbus refer to Native Americans as Indians?
A. Possible Answer Because he thought he had reached the East Indies.

(E)

> **A VOICE FROM THE PAST**
> I presented them with some red caps, and strings of glass beads to wear upon the neck, and many other trifles of small value, wherewith they were much delighted, and became wonderfully attached to us. Afterwards they came swimming to the boats where we were, bringing parrots, balls of cotton thread, javelins, and many other things which they exchanged for the articles we gave them . . . in fact they accepted anything and gave what they had with the utmost good will.
> **CHRISTOPHER COLUMBUS,** *Journal of Columbus*

(F)

This portrait of Christopher Columbus was painted by the Spanish artist Pedro Berruguete, who lived at the same time. It is believed to be the most accurate depiction of the Italian sea captain.

Columbus, however, had miscalculated where he was. He had not reached the East Indies. Scholars believe he landed instead on an island in the Bahamas in the Caribbean Sea. The natives there were not Indians, but a group who called themselves the Taino. Nonetheless, Columbus claimed the island for Spain. He named it San Salvador, or "Holy Savior."

Columbus, like other explorers, was interested in gold. Finding none on San Salvador, he explored other islands throughout the Caribbean, staking his claim to each one. "It was my wish to bypass no island without taking possession," he wrote.

In early 1493, Columbus returned to Spain. The reports he relayed about his journey delighted the Spanish monarchs. Spain's rulers, who had funded his first voyage, agreed

The Atlantic World **483**

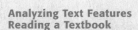

Reading a Chart

Charts summarize information in an organized way for easy reference and comparison. The following tips can help you read a chart quickly and accurately. Refer to the example as you read each strategy.

A Look at the **title** to find out the content of the chart.

B Read the **introduction** to get a general overview of the information included in the chart.

C Examine the **heading** of each row and column. To find specific information, locate the place where a row and column intersect.

A **It's All Downhill: Recreational v. Speed Skiing**

B This chart shows statistics for two skiers in Bariloche, Argentina.

Time (seconds)	Distance traveled (feet)	
	Recreational skier	Speed skier
10	220	2040
20	440	4080
30	660	6120
40	880	8160

C

‖MARK IT UP⟩ Use the chart to answer the following questions.

1. What is the purpose of this chart?

_____

2. After 20 seconds, how far has the speed skier traveled? Circle the answer in the chart.

3. How would you determine each skier's speed in feet per second?

_____

4. About how many times faster than the recreational skier is the speed skier traveling?

_____

5. Which skier's distance is increasing more rapidly?

_____

Reading a Map

To read a map correctly, you have to identify and understand its elements. Look at the map as you read each strategy in this list.

A Read the **title** to understand the content of the map.

B Study the **legend,** or **key,** to find out what the symbols and colors on the map stand for.

C Look at **geographic labels** to understand specific places on the map.

D Locate the **compass rose,** or **pointer,** to determine direction.

E Look at the **scale** to understand what each unit of measurement on the map represents in real distance.

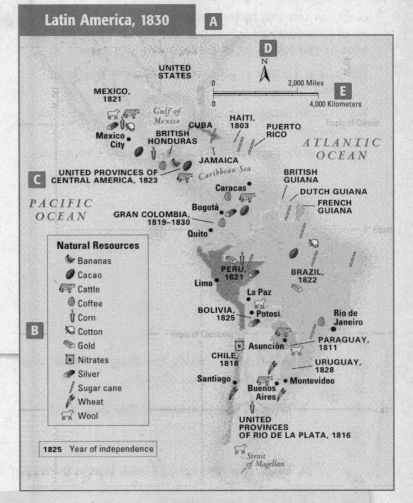

Latin America, 1830 **A**

Natural Resources
- Bananas
- Cacao
- Cattle
- Coffee
- Corn
- Cotton
- Gold
- Nitrates
- Silver
- Sugar cane
- Wheat
- Wool

1825 Year of independence

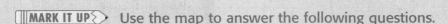

MARK IT UP Use the map to answer the following questions.

1. What does this map show? _____

_____

2. Which country has the greatest number of different natural resources?

_____

3. Put a check mark next to the country that produces the most sugar cane.

4. What is the year of independence of Bolivia?

_____

Reading a Diagram

Diagrams combine pictures with a few words to provide a
lot of information. Look at the example on the opposite
page as you read each of the following strategies.

A Look at the **title** to get an idea of what the diagram is
about.

B Study the **images** closely to understand each part of the
diagram.

C Look at the **captions** and the **labels** for more information.

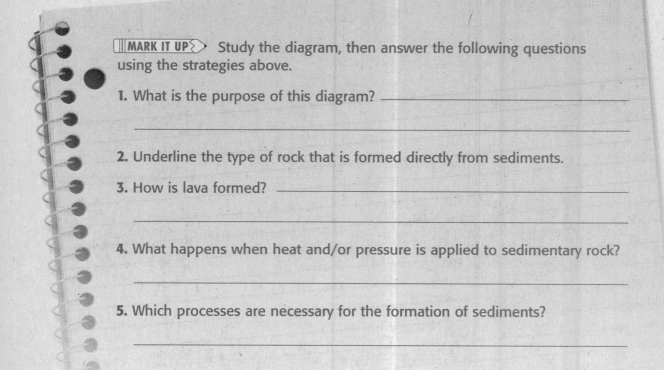

MARK IT UP Study the diagram, then answer the following questions
using the strategies above.

1. What is the purpose of this diagram? _____

_____

2. Underline the type of rock that is formed directly from sediments.

3. How is lava formed? _____

_____

4. What happens when heat and/or pressure is applied to sedimentary rock?

_____

5. Which processes are necessary for the formation of sediments?

_____

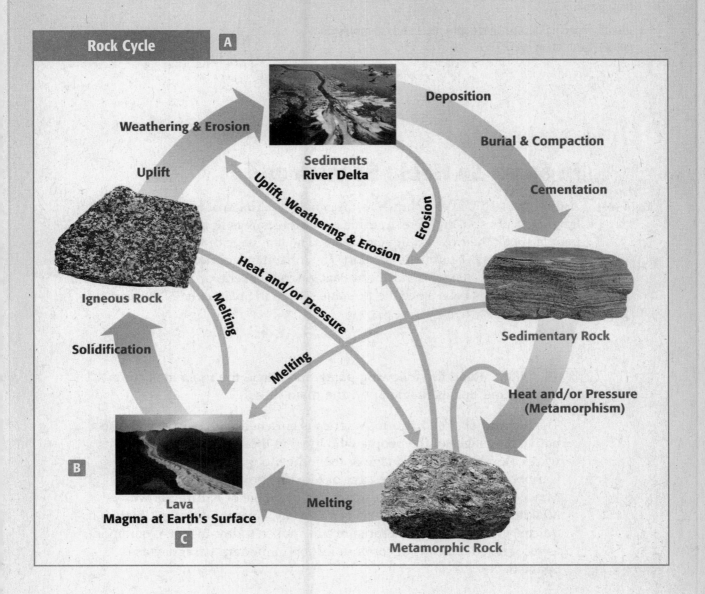

Rock Cycle A

Deposition

Weathering & Erosion

Burial & Compaction

Uplift

Cementation

Sediments
River Delta

Erosion

Uplift, Weathering & Erosion

Heat and/or Pressure

Igneous Rock

Melting

Solidification

Melting

Sedimentary Rock

Melting

Heat and/or Pressure
(Metamorphism)

B

Lava
Magma at Earth's Surface

C

Melting

Metamorphic Rock

Main Idea and Supporting Details

The *main idea* of a paragraph is its most important point. Details in the paragraph support the main idea. Identifying the main idea will help you focus on the main message the writer wants to communicate. Use the following strategies to help you identify a paragraph's main idea and supporting details.

- Look for the **main idea,** which is often the first sentence in a paragraph.

- Use the main idea to help you **summarize** the point of the paragraph.

- Identify specific **details,** including facts and examples, that **support** the main idea.

In Spain Se Habla Spanish and . . .

Main idea

Although Castilian, or Spanish, is the official language of Spain, several other languages are spoken there. In three geographic areas of the country, the people speak their own unique tongues. The language of the part of eastern Spain known as Cataluña is Catalán. The inhabitants of northwest Spain, or Galicia, speak Gallego. In northern País Vasco, Euskera, or Vascuence is still spoken, as it has been since the Romans settled in Spain over 2,200 years ago.

Details

MARK IT UP > Read the following paragraph. Circle the main idea. Then underline three details that support the main idea.

The Spanish spoken in Latin America is enriched with words from the native languages of the people who lived in those countries before they were colonized. The language of the indigenous peoples of the Caribbean was Taíno. The Aztecs of Mexico spoke Náhuatl and the Maya of Guatemala, Maya-quiché. The language of Nicaragua was Miskito; of Peru, Quechua; and of Paraguay, Guaraní. Náhuatl, Maya-quiché, Quechua, and Guaraní are still spoken today. In fact, Guaraní is as recognized a means of communication in modern Paraguay as is Spanish.

Problem and Solution

Does the proposed solution to a problem make sense? In order to decide, you need to look at each part of the text. Use the following strategies to read the text below.

- Look at the beginning or middle of a paragraph to find the **statement of the problem.**

- Find **details** that explain the problem and tell why it is important.

- Look for the **proposed solution.**

- Identify the **supporting details** for the proposed solution.

- Think about whether the solution is a good one.

If You Can't Read This, We Can Help

by Ariel Sánchez

Statement of a problem

According to the cover story in the latest *Westside Weekly*, almost 20% of the junior class is reading at or below the fifth-grade level. Some of these students are having trouble because English is their second language. Others are just casualties of our educational system whose special needs were never recognized. If these students don't somehow dramatically improve their skills, they will lose their chance to become productive members of society.

Explanation of problem

The students in my English class decided to address this problem by setting up a tutoring center. The administration has given us permission to use our classroom after school hours. Our English teacher and one of the Spanish teachers have offered to train tutors, provide materials, and serve as consultants.

We think that this is an ideal solution to the problem for several reasons. First, poor readers are more likely to admit their problem and accept help from their peers. They will receive the individualized help they need in a nonjudgmental setting. Second, the tutoring sessions will be kept private. There will be no stigma attached to attending. Finally, tutors will have a chance to hone their own skills.

You don't have to read between the lines to see that this is a win-win solution to a serious problem.

⫾⫾MARK IT UP⫽ Use the text and strategies above to answer these questions.

1. Circle the proposed solution.

2. Underline at least one detail that supports the solution.

3. Explain why you think this is or is not a good solution to the problem.

_____

_____

Sequence

Understanding the *sequence*, or order of events, in what you read can help you learn what happens and why. The tips below can help you identify sequence in any type of text.

- Read through the passage and identify its **main steps** or stages.

- Look for **words and phrases that signal time,** such as *August 24, 1899, in 1921,* and *at noon.*

- Look for **words and phrases that signal order,** such as *after he graduated, the next year,* and *now.*

|||MARK IT UP⟩ Read the passage about Jorge Luis Borges on the next page. Then use the information from the article and the tips above to answer the questions.

1. Circle words or phrases in the article that signal time.

2. Underline the phrases that signal order.

3. A flow chart can help you understand the sequence of events. Use information from the article to complete this flow chart.

> **Borges immerses himself in languages.**
>
> His first language is _____.

↓

> **He writes his first book in Spanish.**
>
> This book of poems, _____,
> is published in 1923.

↓

> **He expands his literary talents.**
>
> He delves into his inner world of _____.

↓

> **Borges continues writing after going blind.**
>
> In 1980, he is awarded Spain's prestigious_____.

Jorge Luis Borges: A Labyrinth of a Life

Argentinean writer and poet Jorge Luis Borges was born into a wealthy Buenos Aires family on August 24, 1899. Having both a grandmother and a governess who were British, he learned English before he learned Spanish. It was always assumed that Borges would become a writer.

He began writing and translating as a child and continued to expand his command of languages while his family was in Switzerland during World War I. Borges went to high school in Geneva, where he studied Latin, German, and French. After he graduated, he attended Cambridge University in England.

Moving to Spain with his family in 1919, Borges joined a group of writers called the Ultraists. He wrote essays and poetry in English and French as well as Spanish during that time. It was his return to Argentina in 1921, however, that provided the emotion, the material—and the language—for his first published work. His book of poems *Fervor de Buenos Aires—The Passion of Buenos Aires*—appeared in 1923.

Borges continued developing as a writer, exploring his inner world of fantasy and dreams, and blurring the distinctions between prose and poetry.

Ironically, just as his artistic vision was blossoming, he began losing his sight. By 1955, he was totally blind. To keep writing, he relied on dictation.

Borges' first books to be translated into his first language, English, were *Ficciones* and *Labyrinths*, both published in 1962. Borges won Spain's most prestigious literary award, the Cervantes Prize, in 1980. He died in Switzerland on June 14, 1986.

In the final words of his poem, "Elegy," Borges summarizes the labyrinthine path of his life:

"Oh destiny of Borges, perhaps no stranger than your own."

Cause and Effect

A *cause* is an event that brings about another event. An *effect* is something that happens as a result of the first event. Identifying causes and effects helps you understand how events are related. Use the tips below to find causes and effects in any kind of reading.

- Look for an action or event that answers the question, "What happened?" This is the **effect.**

- Look for an action or event that answers the question, "Why did this happen?" This is the **cause.**

- Look for words or phrases that **signal** causes and effects, such as *because, as a result, therefore, consequently,* and *since.*

MARK IT UP Read the cause-and-effect passage on the next page. Then use the strategies above to help you answer the following questions.

1. Circle the words in the passage that signal causes and effects. The first one has been done for you.

2. What was the overall impact of the Columbian Exchange?

_____

3. Complete the following diagram detailing the positive and negative effects of the Columbian Exchange.

Cause: The Columbian Exchange

Negative Effects:

Positive Effects:

The Columbian Exchange

The arrival of the Spanish in the Americas brought more than a clash of peoples and cultures. It also brought a movement of plants, animals, and diseases between the Eastern and Western Hemispheres. This movement of living things between hemispheres is called the Columbian Exchange.

One result of the Columbian Exchange was the transfer of germs from Europe to the Americas. When Europeans came to America, they brought with them germs that caused diseases such as smallpox, measles, and influenza. Native Americans had no immunity to these germs. Therefore, they died.

Although exact numbers are unknown, historians estimate that the diseases brought by Europeans killed more than 20 million Native Americans in Mexico in the first century after conquest. Many scholars agree that the population of Native Americans in Central America decreased by 90 to 95 percent between the years of 1519 and 1619. The consequences were similar in Peru and other parts of the Americas.

Other effects of the Columbian exchange were more positive. The Spanish brought many plants and animals to the Americas. European livestock—cattle, pigs, and horses—adapted well to life in the Americas. Crops from the Eastern Hemisphere, such as grapes, onions, and wheat, also thrived in the West.

The Columbian Exchange benefited Europe, too. Many American crops became part of the European diet. Two that had a huge impact were potatoes and corn. Because they are highly nutritious, they helped feed European populations that might otherwise have gone hungry. Potatoes, for example, became an important food in Ireland, Russia, and other parts of northern Europe. Without potatoes, Europe's population might not have grown as rapidly as it did.

By mixing the products of two hemispheres, the Columbian Exchange brought the world closer together.

Comparison and Contrast

Comparing two things means showing how they are the same. *Contrasting* two things means showing how they are different. Comparisons and contrasts are often used in science and history books to make a subject clearer. Use these tips to help you understand comparison and contrast in reading assignments such as the article on the opposite page.

- Look for **direct statements** of comparison and contrast. "These things are similar because..." or "One major difference is..."

- Pay attention to **words and phrases that signal comparisons**, such as *also, both, is the same as,* and *in the same way.*

- Notice **words and phrases that signal contrasts**. Some of these are *however, still, but,* and *in contrast.*

MARK IT UP Read the article on the next page. Then use the information from that article and the tips above to answer the questions.

1. Circle the words and phrases that signal comparisons, such as the sample.

2. Underline the words and phrases that signal contrasts. One has been done for you.

3. A chart can help you compare and contrast the characteristics of two subjects. Complete this chart about tortilla and potato chips, using information from the article on the next page.

Characteristics	Tortilla chips	Potato chips
Main ingredient	Corn	
Calories from fat		
Sodium		
Protein		
Options		Sweet potatoes, various flavors

CHOOSE YOUR CHIP

Tortilla and potato chips are top snack choices among Americans of all ages. Some snackers are happy munching on anything salty that crunches. Others are devoted fans of one chip or the other. Here's a look at some facts about these popular snacks.

While tortilla chips are made from corn, potato chips are made from—you guessed it, potatoes. Both chips are traditionally prepared by frying in vegetable oil with lots of salt, although baked versions are also available. Surprisingly, tortilla chips are lighter than potato chips. A 1-oz. serving includes about 17% more tortilla chips than potato chips—24 as opposed to 20.

Neither snack is featured in weight-loss diets, and for good reason. Both chips are loaded with calories and fat.

Although both chips are salty, tortilla chips are relatively less so. A serving of either tortilla or potato chips contains a few grams of protein—not much considering that the same amount of dry cereal has about three times that much. Then again, people choose chips for their taste and texture, not their food value.

As for taste, devotees of both chips have numerous flavor options. Tortilla chip lovers can choose chips made from blue corn or seasoned with salsa, nacho spices, ranch dressing, or guacamole. Similarly, potato chips come made from sweet potatoes or in barbecue, cheese, sour-cream-and-onion, or salt-and-vinegar flavors, to name just a few possibilities. The choices are copious, and up to you. But don't forget, chips are only a tasty snack. People should not eat them in excess or use them to replace a good balanced diet.

TORTILLA CHIPS

Nutrition Facts

Serving Size 1 oz. (28g/About 24 chips)
Servings Per Container About 14

Amount per Serving

Calories 140   Calories from Fat 70

	% Daily Value*
Total Fat 8g	12%
Saturated Fat 1g	6%
Trans Fat 0g	**
Cholesterol 0mg	0%
Sodium 110mg	5%
Total Carbohydrate 17g	6%
Dietary Fiber 1g	4%
Sugars 0g	
Protein 2g	

* Percent Daily Values are based on a 2,000 calorie diet.

INGREDIENTS: White Corn, Vegetable Oil (Contains One or More of the Following: Corn, Sunflower, or Soybean Oil), and Salt.

POTATO CHIPS

Nutrition Facts

Serving Size 1 oz. (28g/About 20 chips)
Servings Per Container About 3

Amount per Serving

Calories 150   Calories from Fat 90

	% Daily Value*
Total Fat 10g	15%
Saturated Fat 3g	15%
Trans Fat 0g	**
Cholesterol 0mg	0%
Sodium 180mg	8%
Total Carbohydrate 15g	5%
Dietary Fiber 1g	4%
Sugars 0g	
Protein 2g	

* Percent Daily Values are based on a 2,000 calorie diet.

INGREDIENTS: Potatoes, Corn and/or Cottonseed Oil, and Salt.

Persuasion

A *persuasion* is an opinion that is backed up with reasons and facts. After you carefully read an opinion and the reasons and facts that support it, you will be able to decide if the opinion makes sense. As you read these tips, look at the sample persuasion on the next page.

- Look for words or phrases that **signal** an **opinion,** such as *I believe, I think, in my opinion,* and *disagree.*

- Identify reasons, facts, or expert opinions that **support** the persuasion.

- Ask yourself if the argument and the reasons that back it up make **sense.**

- Look for **errors in reasoning,** such as overgeneralizations, that may affect the persuasion.

MARK IT UP ⟩ Read the persuasion on the following page. Then use the strategies above to help you answer the following questions.

1. Circle any words or phrases that signal an opinion.

2. Underline any words or phrases that signal the writer's opinion.

3. The writer presents both sides of this persuasion. List the points supporting each side in the chart below.

Language requirement should be increased	Language requirement should not be increased
Knowledge of foreign language a necessary life skill	

Let's Raise the Language Requirement

by Luis Loma

Español
Italiano
Français
Deutch

In our increasingly multicultural world, it's essential for people to be able to understand and communicate in more than one language. Our school currently requires students to complete two years of a foreign language. Although that provides a good foundation, I think the language requirement should be raised to three years.

Learning a foreign language is difficult for many students. It may require memorizing a whole new alphabet as well as unfamiliar vocabulary, grammar, and pronunciation. Foreign language students do not just have to learn facts, as in their other academic classes. In addition, they must use their knowledge of the language to communicate in both speaking and writing. In my opinion, these additional skills are not only quantitatively more demanding than those needed in other classes. They are also qualitatively different and more challenging.

For these reasons, I believe that two years of foreign language study is not long enough to give most students basic competence. In fact, statistics show that only 30% of students taking advanced placement foreign language tests receive college credit for their high school work. An additional year of study would allow students to become more comfortable with and fluent in the language. Those who plan to go on to college would get an academic boost. Those who do not would have gained an important life skill.

Several students I talked with disagree with my point of view. They say that other subjects are more important to them than foreign languages. They plan to pursue other academic majors and could use the extra year to take a science, a history, or an art course. Some teachers expressed concern that their workloads would increase.

As I see it, these objections are not as important as making sure that students get the best and most relevant education the school can provide. An additional year of language study would go a long way toward making this goal a reality.

Social Studies

Social studies class becomes easier when you understand how your textbook's words, pictures, and maps work together to give you information. Following these tips can make you a better reader of social studies lessons. As you read the tips, look at the sample lesson on the right-hand page.

A Look at any **headings** or **subheads** on the page. These give you an idea what the lesson is about.

B Make sure you know the meaning of any boldfaced or underlined **vocabulary terms.** These items often appear on tests.

C Notice **how information is organized.** Social studies books are often organized by chronological order, cause and effect, comparison and contrast, and main idea and supporting details.

D Carefully examine **visuals** and **captions.** Ask yourself how they relate to the text.

E Notice any **special features,** such as extended quotations, questions in the margins, or text in a tinted box. These features extend your understanding of the topic.

MARK IT UP Carefully read the textbook page at right. Use the information from the text and from the tips above to answer the questions.

1. Circle the main idea of this lesson.

2. Draw a box around the vocabulary terms that will be defined in this lesson.

3. How is the information in the two paragraphs at the bottom of the page organized, by main idea and supporting details or by comparison and contrast?

_____

4. Put a check mark by the caption on this page.

5. In addition to the text in One American's Story, which three features give more information about José Martí?

_____

_____

② The Spanish- Ⓐ American War Ⓑ

MAIN IDEA	WHY IT MATTERS NOW
Independence movements in Spanish colonies led to the Spanish-American War in 1898.	U.S. involvement in Latin America and Asia expanded greatly after the Spanish-American War.

ONE AMERICAN'S STORY

José Martí was forced to leave Cuba in the 1870s, when he was still a teenager. In those years, the Caribbean island was a Spanish colony, and he had spoken out for independence. Martí later described the Ⓔ terrible conditions that existed under Spanish rule.

> *A VOICE FROM THE PAST*
>
> Cuba's children . . . suffer in indescribable bitterness as they see their fertile nation enchained and also their human dignity stifled . . . all for the necessities and vices of the [Spanish] monarchy.
>
> **José Martí,** quoted in *José Martí, Mentor of the Cuban Nation*

Ⓓ José Martí dedicated his life to the Cuban struggle for independence from Spain.

After being forced out of Cuba, Martí spent much of his life in the United States. In 1892, he was elected to lead the Cuban Revolutionary Party. At the Party's headquarters in New York City, Martí began to plan a revolt against Spain that began in 1895.

Martí's lifelong struggle for Cuban independence made him a symbol of liberty throughout Latin America. In this section, you will read how U.S. disapproval of Spain's treatment of Cubans led to the Spanish-American War.

Rebellion Against Spain

The Spanish empire was crumbling at the end of the 19th century. Spain had once controlled most of the Americas, including land that became part of the United States. By the 1890s, however, it owned only a few colonies. Among them were the Philippine Islands in the Pacific and the Caribbean Ⓒ islands of Cuba and Puerto Rico. (See the maps on page 665.) Many of the inhabitants of these colonies had begun to demand independence.

Cubans had revolted against Spain several times in the second half of the nineteenth century. Each time, Spanish soldiers defeated the rebels. In 1895, an ongoing economic depression had increased Cubans' anger over Spanish rule, and they rebelled again. José Martí, who had helped to organize the rebellion from New York, returned to Cuba. He was killed in a skirmish with Spanish troops shortly after, but the revolt continued.

Science

Reading a science textbook becomes easier when you understand how the explanations, drawings, and special terms work together. Use the strategies below to help you better understand your science textbook. Look at the examples on the opposite page as you read each strategy in this list.

A Preview the **title** and any **headings** to see what scientific concepts you will learn about.

B Read the **key ideas, objectives**, or **focus.** These items summarize the lesson and help set a purpose for your reading.

C Notice the **boldfaced** and **italicized** terms in the text. Look for the definitions of these terms.

D Carefully examine any **pictures, diagrams,** or **charts.** Read the **titles** and **captions** to see how the graphics help to illustrate the text.

E Look for places that discuss **scientific concepts** in terms of **everyday events** or **experiences.** Think about how these explanations improve your understanding.

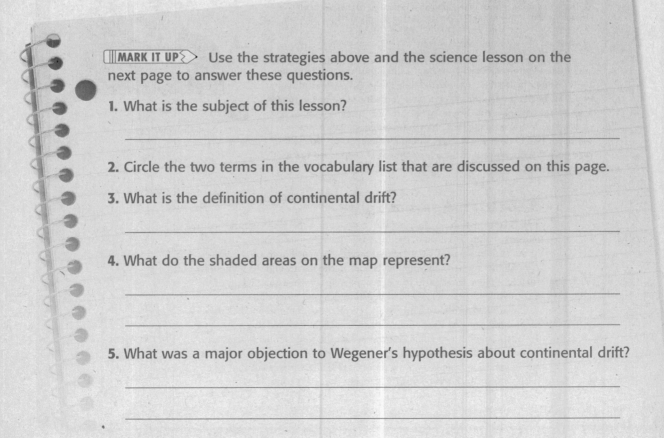

MARK IT UP Use the strategies above and the science lesson on the next page to answer these questions.

1. What is the subject of this lesson?

_____

2. Circle the two terms in the vocabulary list that are discussed on this page.

3. What is the definition of continental drift?

_____

4. What do the shaded areas on the map represent?

_____

_____

5. What was a major objection to Wegener's hypothesis about continental drift?

_____

_____

8.1

B KEY IDEA

The lithosphere is broken into rigid plates that move in relationship to one another on the asthenosphere.

KEY VOCABULARY
- plate tectonics
- continental drift
- mid-ocean ridge

A # What Is Plate Tectonics?

Earth's lithosphere is broken into plates that move on the asthenosphere. In some places, the plates are moving toward each other. In other places, they are moving apart, and in others, they are sliding past each other. **C** **Plate tectonics** (tehk-TAHN-ihks) is a theory that describes the formation, movements, and interactions of these plates.

A ## Early Ideas About Plate Movements

The idea that Earth's surface might be moving is not new. The theory of plate tectonics developed from early observations made about the shapes of the continents and from fossil and climate evidence.

In the early 1500s, explorers using maps noted the remarkable fit of the shape of the west coast of Africa and the shape of the east coast of South America. In 1596, a Dutch mapmaker suggested that the two continents may have been part of a larger continent that had broken apart.

In 1912, a German scientist named Alfred Wegener (VAY-guh-nuhr) proposed a hypothesis called **continental drift.** According to this hypothesis, the continents have moved, or drifted, from one location to another over time. Wegener used many observations to support his hypothesis. In addition to the similarities in the shapes of the continents, he noted that the fossil remains of *Mesosaurus,* a reptile that lived about 270 million years ago, are found only in parts of South America and Africa. This strange distribution is easily explained if the two continents were once joined, as suggested by the map below. Distinctive rock formations found on both continents would have matched up with each other if the continents had been joined in the past. Climate change evidence further supports the continental drift hypothesis.

One of the strongest objections to Wegener's hypothesis was that it did not explain *how* the continents moved. Wegener suggested that the continents might float on deeper, more fluid layers, and that Earth's internal heat could provide the energy needed to move the continents through these layers. He had no evidence to support that explanation, however. Scientists continued to debate Wegener's ideas about continental drift for a number of years. During his lifetime, Wegener continued his efforts to defend the continental drift hypothesis, but he was not successful.

MAP *Mesosaurus* fossils have been found in South America and Africa, lending support to the hypothesis that the continents were once joined together.

D

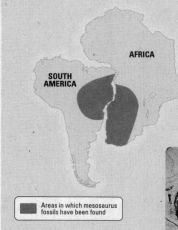

AFRICA

SOUTH AMERICA

Areas in which mesosaurus fossils have been found

FOSSIL EVIDENCE This fossil *Mesosaurus* was found in Brazil. Similar fossils have been found in Africa. **E**

Mathematics

Reading in mathematics is different from reading in history, literature, or science. A math lesson has few words, but instead illustrates math concepts using numbers, symbols, formulas, equations, diagrams, and word problems. Use the following strategies, and the lesson on the next page, to help you better understand your math textbook.

A Preview the **title** and **headings** to see which math concepts you will learn about.

B Find and read the **goals** or **objectives** for the lesson. These will tell the most important points to know.

C Read **explanations** carefully. Sometimes a concept is explained in more than one way to make sure you understand it.

D Study any **worked-out solutions** to sample problems. These are the key to understanding how to do the homework assignment.

E Notice **special features,** such as study or vocabulary hints. These provide more help or information.

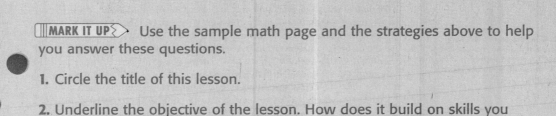

MARK IT UP Use the sample math page and the strategies above to help you answer these questions.

1. Circle the title of this lesson.

2. Underline the objective of the lesson. How does it build on skills you already have learned?

_____

_____

3. What must you do when multiplying or dividing each side of an inequality by a negative number?

_____

4. What process does the example problem demonstrate?

_____

5. What suggestion does the marginal note provide to help you learn this skill?

_____

A Solving Inequalities Using Multiplication or Division

BEFORE	▶ Now	WHY?
You solved equations using multiplication or division.	You'll solve inequalities using multiplication or division.	So you can find how many students must attend a dance, as in Ex. 26.

B

In the Real World

Bats About 15,000 fruit-eating bats live on Panama's Barro Colorado Island. Every year they consume up to 61,440,000 grams of fruit. About how many grams of fruit does each bat consume in a year? You will use an inequality to solve this in Example 3.

There is one important difference between solving inequalities and solving equations. When multiplying or dividing each side of

C an inequality by a negative number, you must *reverse the direction of the inequality symbol.*

Multiplication Property of Inequality

Words	Algebra
Multiplying each side of an inequality by a *positive* number makes an equivalent inequality.	If $4x < 10$, then $\left(\frac{1}{4}\right)(4x) < \left(\frac{1}{4}\right)(10)$.
Multiplying each side of an inequality by a *negative* number and *reversing the direction of the inequality symbol* makes an equivalent inequality.	If $-5x < 10$, then $\left(-\frac{1}{5}\right)(-5x) > \left(-\frac{1}{5}\right)(10)$.

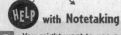

HELP with **Notetaking**

E You might want to use a table to organize this information about reversing the inequality symbol.

D **EXAMPLE 1** Solving an Inequality Using Multiplication

$$-\frac{1}{8}n \geq 2 \qquad \text{Original inequality}$$

$$-8 \cdot \left(-\frac{1}{8}\right)n \leq -8 \cdot 2 \qquad \begin{array}{l}\text{Multiply each side by } -8.\\ \text{Reverse inequality symbol.}\end{array}$$

$$n \leq -16 \qquad \text{Simplify.}$$

Reading an Application

To get a part-time job or to register for summer camp or classes at the local community center, you will have to fill out an application. Being able to understand the format of an application will help you fill it out correctly. Use the following strategies and the sample on the next page to help you understand any application.

A **Begin at the top.** Scan the application to understand the different sections.

B Look for special **instructions for filling** out the application.

C Note any **request for materials** that must be included with the application.

D Pay attention to **optional sections,** or **those sections you don't have to fill in.**

E Look for difficult or confusing words or abbreviations. Look them up in a dictionary or ask someone what they mean.

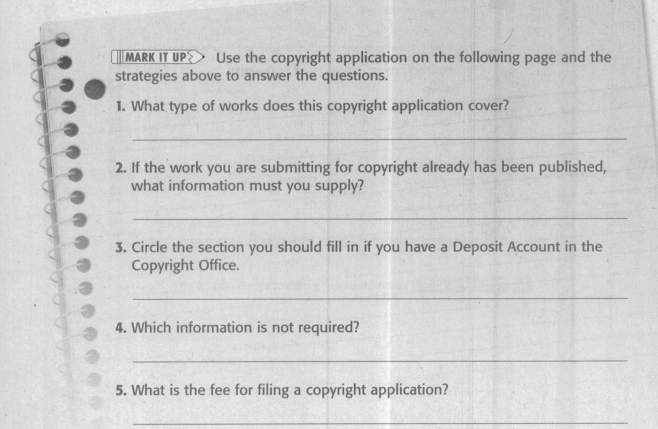

MARK IT UP Use the copyright application on the following page and the strategies above to answer the questions.

1. What type of works does this copyright application cover?

   _____

2. If the work you are submitting for copyright already has been published, what information must you supply?

   _____

3. Circle the section you should fill in if you have a Deposit Account in the Copyright Office.

   _____

4. Which information is not required?

   _____

5. What is the fee for filing a copyright application?

   _____

6. **ASSESSMENT PRACTICE** Circle the letter of the correct answer. How many copies of an unpublished work must accompany the application?
   A. none   **B.** one   **C.** two   **D.** three

SHORT FORM TX

For a Nondramatic Literary Work

UNITED STATES COPYRIGHT OFFICE

Registration Number

TYPE OR PRINT IN BLACK INK. DO NOT WRITE ABOVE THIS LINE. [B]

[A]

Examined By _____

Correspondence _____

Title of This Work: Alternative title or title of larger work in which this work was published:	**1**	
Name and Address of Author and Owner of the Copyright: Nationality or domicile: Phone, fax, and email:	**2**	Phone (___) _____ Fax (___) _____ Email _____
Year of Creation:	**3**	
***If work has been published,* Date and Nation of Publication:**	**4**	a. Date _____ Month Day Year b. Nation _____ *(Month, day, and year all required)*
Type of Authorship in This Work: Check all that this author created.	**5**	❑ Text (includes fiction, nonfiction, poetry, computer programs, etc.) ❑ Illustrations ❑ Photographs ❑ Compilation of terms or data
Signature: Registration cannot be completed without a signature.	**6**	*I certify that the statements made by me in this application are correct to the best of my knowledge.* Check one: ❑ Author ❑ Authorized agent X _____
[D] OPTIONAL **Name and Address of Person to Contact for Rights and Permissions:** Phone, fax, and email:	**7**	❑ Check here if same as #2 above. Phone (___) _____ Fax (___) _____ Email _____

8

Certificate will be mailed in window envelope to this address:

Name _____

Number/Street/Apt. [E] _____

_____

City _____

State/ZIP _____

Complete this space only if you currently hold a Deposit Account in the Copyright Office.

9

Deposit Account # _____

Name _____

_____

_____

DO NOT WRITE HERE   Page 1 of _____ pages

━━━━━━━━━━━━━━ MAIL WITH THE FORM ━━━━━━━━━━━━━━

- A $30 filing fee in the form of a check or money order (*no cash*) payable to "Register of Copyrights,"

[C]   **and**

- One or two copies of the work. If the work is unpublished, send one copy. If published, send two copies of the best published edition. (If first published outside the U.S., send one copy either as first published or of the best edition.)
Note: Inquire about special requirements for works first published before 1978. Copies submitted become the property of the U.S. Government.

Mail everything **(application form, copy or copies, and fee)** *in one package* to:
    Library of Congress/Copyright Office
    101 Independence Avenue, S.E.
    Washington, D.C. 20559-6000

Reading a Public Notice

Public notices can tell you about events in your community and give you valuable information about safety. When you read a public notice, follow these tips. Each tip relates to a specific part of the notice on the next page.

A Read the notice's **title,** if it has one. The title often gives the main idea or purpose of the notice.

B See if there is a logo, credit, or other way of telling **who created the notice.**

C Search for information that explains **who should read the notice.**

D Look for **instructions**—things the notice is asking or telling you to do.

E See if there are details that tell you how to **find out more** about the topic.

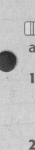

MARK IT UP Use the public notice on the next page and the strategies above to answer the questions.

1. What organization sponsored this notice?

_____

2. Who is the intended audience of this notice?

_____

3. When should comments and requests for hearing be received?

_____

4. Where and when may documents about this issue be inspected and copied?

_____

5. Circle the name of the person you should contact for more information about this issue.

6. ASSESSMENT PRACTICE Circle the letter of the correct answer.
Controllers Inc. has applied for permission to
   A. comment on water pollution in Massachusetts.
   B. receive a tax reduction for contributing to the OEP.
   C. discharge materials into Massachusetts waters.
   D. advertise its company's services publicly.

Public Notice

Notice No. MAF: 00001234.jlb

Public Notice Beginning Date: January 10, 2003
Public Notice Ending Date: February 10, 2003

A **National Pollutant Discharge Elimination System (NPDES) Permit Program**

PUBLIC NOTICE/FACT SHEET
of
Draft Reissued NPDES Permit to Discharge into Waters of the State

Public Notice/Fact Sheet Issued By:
B OEP
Division of Water Pollution Control
Permit Section, 1234 Main St.
Springfield, Massachusetts
800-555-1212

Name and Address of Discharger:
Christopher Land, Owner
Controllers, Inc.
4321 Lee Way
Springfield, MA

Name and Address of Facility:
Controllers Inc. Plant
Route 90 Exit 4
Springfield, MA

The Organization of Environmental Protection (OEP) has made a tentative determination to issue a NPDES Permit to discharge into the waters of the state and has prepared a draft Permit and associated fact sheet for the above named discharger. The Public Notice period will begin and end on the dates indicated in the heading of this Public Notice/Fact Sheet. Interested persons are invited **D** to submit written comments on the draft Permit to the OEP at the above address. Persons submitting comments and/or requests for public hearing shall also send a copy of such comments or requests to the Permit applicant.

C The application, engineer's review notes including load limit calculations, Public Notice/Fact Sheet, draft Permit, comments received, and other documents are available for inspection and may be copied at the OEP between 9:30 a.m. and 3:30 p.m. Monday through Friday when scheduled by the interested person.

E For further information, please call Clark Pucci at 800-555-1212.

Reading a Web Page

If you need information for a report, project, or hobby, the World Wide Web can probably help you. The tips below will help you understand the Web pages you read. Look at the sample Web page on the right as you read each of the strategies.

A Notice the page's **Web address,** or URL. You might want to write it down so you can return to the page later.

B Look for **menu bars** along the top, bottom, or side of the page. These guide you to other parts of the site that may be useful.

C Look for **links** to other parts of the site or to related pages. Links are often highlighted in color or underlined.

D Use a **search feature** to quickly find out whether the information you want to locate appears anywhere on the site.

E Many sites have a link that allows you to **contact** the creators with questions or feedback.

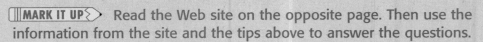 **MARK IT UP** Read the Web site on the opposite page. Then use the information from the site and the tips above to answer the questions.

1. Circle the Web address of this site.

2. Put a check mark by the link you would click to learn more about El Salvador.

3. What is the subject of the feature article?

_____

4. Which article provides information about the difficulties of adjusting to multicultural living?

_____

5. If you needed help using this site, which link would you click on?

_____

6. ASSESSMENT PRACTICE Circle the letter of the correct answer.
How can you get a daily *Orbe News* update?
A. Click on Sign Me Up
B. Click on EMAIL
C. Click on News Summary
D. Watch the news in TV at 11p.m.

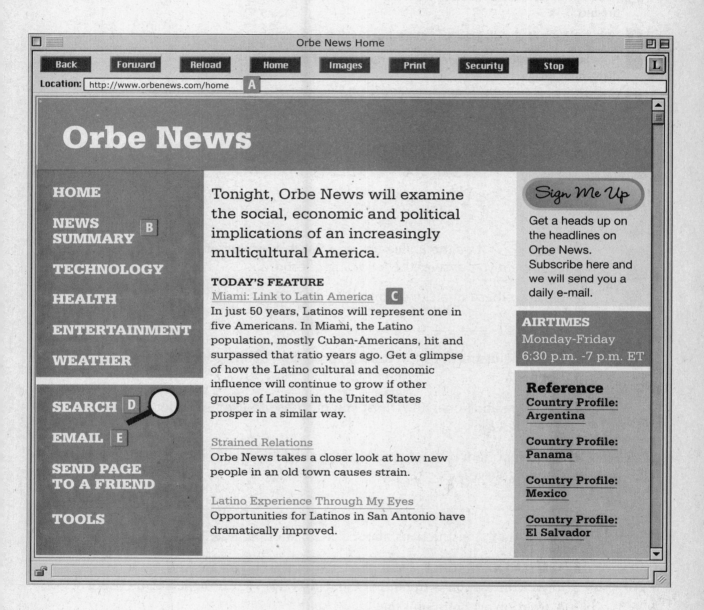

Orbe News Home

Back | Forward | Reload | Home | Images | Print | Security | Stop | L

Location: http://www.orbenews.com/home A

Orbe News

HOME

NEWS SUMMARY B

TECHNOLOGY

HEALTH

ENTERTAINMENT

WEATHER

SEARCH D

EMAIL E

SEND PAGE TO A FRIEND

TOOLS

Tonight, Orbe News will examine the social, economic and political implications of an increasingly multicultural America.

TODAY'S FEATURE

Miami: Link to Latin America C

In just 50 years, Latinos will represent one in five Americans. In Miami, the Latino population, mostly Cuban-Americans, hit and surpassed that ratio years ago. Get a glimpse of how the Latino cultural and economic influence will continue to grow if other groups of Latinos in the United States prosper in a similar way.

Strained Relations

Orbe News takes a closer look at how new people in an old town causes strain.

Latino Experience Through My Eyes

Opportunities for Latinos in San Antonio have dramatically improved.

Sign Me Up

Get a heads up on the headlines on Orbe News. Subscribe here and we will send you a daily e-mail.

AIRTIMES

Monday-Friday

6:30 p.m. -7 p.m. ET

Reference

Country Profile: Argentina

Country Profile: Panama

Country Profile: Mexico

Country Profile: El Salvador

Reading Technical Directions

Reading technical directions will help you understand how to use the products you buy. Use the following tips to help you read a variety of technical directions.

A Scan the **title** and any other important **headings** to understand what topic is being explained.

B **Read all the directions** carefully at least once before using the product.

C Look carefully at any **diagrams** or **other images** of the product.

D Note **labels** or **captions** that identify important parts of the diagram or image.

E Look for **numbers** or **letters** that give the sequence of steps to follow.

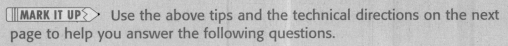 Use the above tips and the technical directions on the next page to help you answer the following questions.

1. What do these directions explain?

_____

2. Circle the instructions for locating the Super Cleaning Valve on the Insect Trapper.

3. Circle the additional item must you purchase to use the Super Cleaning Valve.

4. What important precautions should you take before using the Super Cleaning Valve?

_____

5. Underline the instructions about how to start the flow of CO_2.

6. **ASSESSMENT PRACTICE** Circle the letter of the correct answer.
In which situation is the Super Cleaning Valve NOT designed to be used?
A. to troubleshoot a unit that won't start
B. when a "Gas Empty" fault code has occurred
C. to clear out fuel line contaminants before storing
D. without the L-shaped adaptor

A Super Cleaning Valve

Super Cleaning Valve has been installed to clear out propane contaminants in the fuel line which may block the flow of propane from the tank to your Insect Trapper. Refer to Figure B for valve location on your Insect Trapper.

Recommended for use every two tank changes. The valve should be used when "Gas Empty" signal is present, when unit won't start, and before seasonal storage to avoid build up of contaminants during off-season.

The Super Cleaning Valve should be used with the L-shaped adaptor included with your Insect Trapper and a 12 gram threaded CO_2 cylinder (*Fig. A*) available at any bicycle shop.

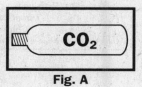
Fig. A

Important: *Extinguish all smoking materials before using Super Cleaning Valve. Use of protective glasses is recommended.*

B Instructions for Use

E 1. Shut off flow of gas from propane tank.

2. Turn off power on Insect Trapper unit.

3. Remove cap from Super Cleaning Valve on your unit (*Fig. B*).

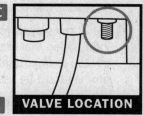
Fig. B

4. Hand-screw L-shaped adaptor on to Super Cleaning Valve, until tight.

5 Hand-screw CO_2 cylinder into L-shaped adaptor.

6. Unscrew CO_2 cylinder 1/4 of a turn. Flow of CO_2 will begin, lasting 5 minutes.

7. Replace valve cap and proceed with normal start up per instructions in your Insect Trapper manual.

Reading Product Information: Directions for Use

Companies are required by law to offer instructions and warnings about the safe use of their products. Learning to read and follow product guidelines is important for your safety. Look at the sample product information as you read the strategies below.

A Scan **headings** to understand what information about the product is included.

B Read information on the **purpose** or **uses** of the product.

C Look closely at **directions** and **recommendations** to ensure safe use of the product.

D Study any **warnings** or other highlighted information that describe specific dangers, side effects, or important conditions under which the product must be used.

E Look for **contact information** that tells you where to call or write if you have a question about the product.

BUG*Gone*
*Kills ants, roaches, crickets, silverfish, and spiders **B**
in the home on contact.*

A **Active Ingredients:**

Permethrin	0.2%	Piperonyl butoxide	0.5%
Pyrethrins	0.2%	Inert ingredients	99.1%

Directions for Use: Shake well before each use. Hold container upright. Do not spray up into air. Apply to surfaces only. Spray until surfaces are wet. Avoid excessive wetting of asphalt, tile, rubber, and plastic. Reapply as necessary. **C**

Storage: Store away from heat or open flames, in an area inaccessible to children.

Disposal: This container can be recycled. Before recycling, empty can completely. DO NOT PUNCTURE. If recycling is not available, replace cap, wrap in newspaper, and discard in trash.

PRECAUTIONARY STATEMENTS:

CAUTION: Harmful if swallowed or absorbed through the skin. Avoid breathing spray mist and contact with hands or clothing. Wash hands after use. **If swallowed:** DO NOT INDUCE VOMITING. Contact a physician or Poison Control Center immediately. **If in eyes:** Flush with plenty of water. **If on skin:** Wash promptly with soap and water. **If inhaled:** Remove victim to fresh air. Apply artificial respiration if indicated. **D**

NOTE TO PHYSICIANS: Product contains petroleum distillate (aspiration hazard).

FLAMMABLE: CONTENTS UNDER PRESSURE. Keep away from heat, sparks, open flame, or pilot lights. Do not puncture or incinerate container. Exposure to temperatures above 130 °F may cause bursting.

Questions? Comments? **E**
Call 800-555-1212

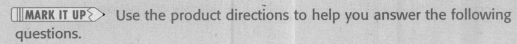

MARK IT UP Use the product directions to help you answer the following questions.

1. Underline the instructions to follow if the product is inhaled.

2. Circle the directions about storing the product.

3. What should you do after using the product?

_____

4. Why should the container not be punctured?

_____

5. ASSESSMENT PRACTICE Circle the letter of the correct answer.
Why would someone purchase this product?

A. to eliminate insects in the garden

B. to kill various household insects

C. to reverse the damage done by termites

D. to protect house plants from infestation

Reading a Recreation Schedule

Knowing how to read a recreation schedule can help you plan events and organize your time wisely. Look at the example as you read each strategy on this list.

A Look at the **title** and other **headings** to know what the schedule covers.

B Identify **labels** that show **dates** or **days of the week** to help you understand how the daily or weekly schedule works.

C Look for **expressions of time** to know what hours or minutes are listed on the schedule.

D Look for specific **locations** or **activities**.

E Look for **changes** or **exceptions** to the regular schedule.

A CO-REC SCHEDULE: September 2–June 6 **E** Note: This schedule is subject to change without notice.			
Day/Area	**M, W, F** **B**	**Tu, Th, Sa**	**Sun**
Main gym	9:00 AM–4:00 PM	10:00 AM–6:00 PM	Noon–7:00 PM
Softball field	Closed	4:00 AM–7:00 PM	Noon–6:00 PM
Student fitness center **D**	6:30 AM–11:00 PM	6:30 AM–11:00 PM	9:00 AM–8:00 PM
Tennis center	3:00 PM–9:00 PM	1:00 PM–7:00 PM	9:00 PM–1:00 PM
Lap pool	Noon–1:30 PM; **C** 7:00 AM–9:00 PM	Noon–1:30 PM; 7:00 AM–9:00 PM	Noon–4:00 PM

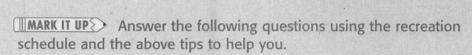 **MARK IT UP** Answer the following questions using the recreation schedule and the above tips to help you.

1. Circle the period of time that is covered by this schedule.

2. At how many different locations are activities scheduled?

_____

3. If you want to play softball, on what days can you use the field?

_____

4. ASSESSMENT PRACTICE Circle the letter of the correct answer. If you work until 4:00 PM on Sundays, what facilities can you use afterwards to help you unwind?

A. student fitness center

B. student fitness center, main gym

C. student fitness center, main gym, softball field

D. student fitness center, main gym, softball field, lap pool

Test Preparation Strategies

In this section you'll find strategies and practice to help you with many different kinds of standardized tests. The strategies apply to questions based on long and short readings, as well as questions about charts, graphs, and product labels. You'll also find examples and practice for revising-and-editing tests and writing tests. Applying the strategies to the practice materials and thinking through the answers will help you succeed in many formal testing situations.

Test Preparation Strategies

You can prepare for tests in several ways. First, study and understand the content that will be on the test. Second, learn as many test-taking techniques as you can. These techniques will help you better understand the questions and how to answer them. Following are some general suggestions for preparing for and taking tests. Starting on page 156, you'll find more detailed suggestions and test-taking practice.

Successful Test Taking

 Study Content Throughout the Year

1. **Master the content of your class.** The best way to study for tests is to read, understand, and review the content of your class. Read your daily assignments carefully. Study the notes that you have taken in class. Participate in class discussions. Work with classmates in small groups to help one another learn. You might trade writing assignments and comment on your classmates' work.

2. **Use your textbook for practice.** Your textbook includes many different types of questions. Some may ask you to talk about a story you just read. Others may ask you to figure out what's wrong with a sentence or how to make a paragraph sound better. Try answering these questions out loud and in writing. This type of practice can make taking a test much easier.

3. **Learn how to understand the information in charts, maps, and graphic organizers.** One type of test question may ask you to look at a graphic organizer, such as a spider map, and explain something about the information you see there. Another type of question may ask you to look at a map to find a particular place. You'll find charts, maps, and graphic organizers to study in your textbook. You'll also find charts, maps, and graphs in your science, mathematics, literature, and social studies textbooks. When you look at these, ask yourself, What information is being presented and why is it important?

4. **Practice taking tests.** Use copies of tests you have taken in the past or in other classes for practice. Every test has a time limit, so set a timer for 15 or 20 minutes and then begin your practice. Try to finish the test in the time you've given yourself.

☑ **Reading Check** In what practical way can your textbook help you prepare for a test?

5. Talk about test-taking experiences. After you've taken a classroom test or quiz, talk about it with your teacher and classmates. Which types of questions were the hardest to understand? What made them difficult? Which questions seemed easiest, and why? When you share test-taking techniques with your classmates, everyone can become a successful test taker.

Use Strategies During the Test

1. Read the directions carefully. You can't be a successful test taker unless you know exactly what you are expected to do. Look for key words and phrases, such as *circle the best answer, write a paragraph,* or *choose the word that best completes each sentence.*

2. Learn how to read test questions. Test questions can sometimes be difficult to figure out. They may include unfamiliar language or be written in an unfamiliar way. Try rephrasing the question in a simpler way using words you understand. Always ask yourself, What type of information does this question want me to provide?

3. Pay special attention when using a separate answer sheet. If you accidentally skip a line on an answer sheet, all the rest of your answers may be wrong! Try one or more of the following techniques:

- Use a ruler on the answer sheet to make sure you are placing your answers on the correct line.

- After every five answers, check to make sure you're on the right line.

- Each time you turn a page of the test booklet, check to make sure the number of the question is the same as the number of the answer line on the answer sheet.

- If the answer sheet has circles, fill them in neatly. A stray pencil mark might cause the scoring machine to count the answer as incorrect.

4. If you're not sure of the answer, make your best guess. Unless you've been told that there is a penalty for guessing, choose the answer that you think is likeliest to be correct.

5. Keep track of the time. Answering all the questions on a test usually results in a better score. That's why finishing the test is important. Keep track of the time you have left. At the beginning of the test, figure out how many questions you will have to answer by the halfway point in order to finish in the time given.

☑ **Reading Check** What are at least two good ways to avoide skipping lines on an answer sheet?

Understand Types of Test Questions

Most tests include two types of questions: multiple choice and open-ended. Specific strategies will help you understand and correctly answer each type of question.

A **multiple-choice question** has two parts. The first part is the question itself, called the stem. The second part is a series of possible answers. Usually four possible answers are provided, and only one of them is correct. Your task is to choose the correct answer. Here are some strategies to help you do just that.

1. Read and think about each question carefully before looking at the possible answers.

2. Pay close attention to key words in the question. For example, look for the word *not*, as in "Which of the following is not a cause of the conflict in this story?"

3. Read and think about all of the possible answers before making your choice.

4. Reduce the number of choices by eliminating any answers you know are incorrect. Then, think about why some of the remaining choices might also be incorrect.

   • If two of the choices are pretty much the same, both are probably wrong.

   • Answers that contain any of the following words are usually incorrect: *always, never, none, all,* and *only.*

5. If you're still unsure about an answer, see if any of the following applies:

   • When one choice is longer and more detailed than the others, it is often the correct answer.

   • When a choice repeats a word that is in the question, it may be the correct answer.

   • When two choices are direct opposites, one of them is likely the correct answer.

   • When one choice includes one or more of the other choices, it is often the correct answer.

   • When a choice includes the word *some* or *often*, it may be the correct answer.

   • If one of the choices is *All of the above*, make sure that at least two of the other choices seem correct.

   • If one of the choices is *None of the above*, make sure that none of the other choices seems correct.

☑ Reading Check What words in a multiple-choice question probably signal a wrong answer?

An **open-ended test item** can take many forms. It might ask you to write a word or phrase to complete a sentence. You might be asked to create a chart, draw a map, or fill in a graphic organizer. Sometimes, you will be asked to write one or more paragraphs in response to a writing prompt. Use the following strategies when reading and answering open-ended items:

1. If the item includes directions, read them carefully. Take note of any steps required.

2. Look for key words and phrases in the item as you plan how you will respond. Does the item ask you to identify a cause-and-effect relationship or to compare and contrast two or more things? Are you supposed to provide a sequence of events or make a generalization? Does the item ask you to write an essay in which you state your point of view and then try to persuade others that your view is correct?

3. If you're going to be writing a paragraph or more, plan your answer. Jot down notes and a brief outline of what you want to say before you begin writing.

4. Focus your answer. Don't include everything you can think of, but be sure to include everything the item asks for.

5. If you're creating a chart or drawing a map, make sure your work is as clear as possible.

☑ **Reading Check** What are at least three key strategies for answering an open-ended question?

READING STRATEGIES FOR ASSESSMENT

Notice the setting. Circle the words that tell you where the story takes place. Is there more than one setting?

Reading Test Model
LONG SELECTIONS

DIRECTIONS Read the following retelling of an Aztec legend. The notes in the side columns will help you prepare for the types of questions that are likely to follow a reading like this. You might want to preview the questions on pages 160 and 161 before you begin reading.

How the Lord of the Winds Brought Music to the Earth

At the beginning of time, Earth was given life by two powerful gods: Tezcatlipoca, called Smoking Mirror, and Quetzalcoatl, the serpent god called Lord of the Winds. Earth was filled with dazzling colors and wondrous forms of life. Sadly, however, Earth had no music. No birdsong filled the morning air. No streams murmured in the hills. No wolves' howls serenaded the midnight moon.

Music existed only in one place—the Palace of the Sun. High above Earth, the Sun's musicians played beautiful melodies day and night. Smoking Mirror was jealous of the Sun's music and vowed to find a way to bring music to Earth.

One day, Smoking Mirror drew in a deep breath and, raising his voice, called mightily for Quetzalcoatl. He called to him in the rolling hills and the tall mountains. He called to him in the flat plains and the low valleys. He called to him in the winding rivers and the deep oceans.

Hearing Smoking Mirror's call, Quetzalcoatl slowly opened his eyes, unwound his serpent coils, and headed toward his friend's voice.

"You'll wake the dead!" the Lord of the Winds thundered when he found Smoking Mirror. "What can possibly be so important that you disturb my pleasant slumber?"

"Look around you," Smoking Mirror demanded. "See the rainbows dancing in the waterfalls? The brightly–painted birds streaking across the sky? Feel the warm soil beneath you? Now, inhale deeply and savor the scents of a thousand wildflowers. Earth is truly a paradise, except for…"

"Except for what?" Quetzalcoatl shouted, his patience wearing thin.

"Earth has no music," Smoking Mirror noted sadly. "You must help me, friend, to bring joyful sounds to this place we created."

"And how exactly do you propose I do that?" Quetzalcoatl inquired.

"Why, you must go to the Palace of the Sun and gather up the Sun's musicians. Carry them back with you. They alone can bring music to Earth," Smoking Mirror said.

The Lord of the Winds sighed and addressed Smoking Mirror. "You know as well as I that the Sun's musicians have pledged to serve him faithfully. They will never consider leaving him to come to Earth."

Smoking Mirror knew that the Lord of the Winds spoke the truth about the Sun's

Understand the purpose. Why did the Aztecs pass this legend down through the generations? What were they trying to explain?

Pay attention to character and relationships. What kind of god is Smoking Mirror? What kind of god is Quetzalcoatl? How would you describe their relationship?

Identify the climax. The climax is the most important moment or emotional high point of a story.

musicians. At the same time, the Lord of the Winds knew that Smoking Mirror spoke the truth about the need for music on Earth. So Quetzalcoatl began his journey to the heavens, thinking as he went about how to get the Sun's musicians to join him on Earth.

Looking out from his palace, the Sun spied the Lord of the Winds as he made his way up through the sky. Quickly, he gathered his musicians around him and told them they must cease their music immediately lest the Lord of the Winds hear them and carry them away to Earth. Earth, he reminded them, was a terribly dark and silent place.

Quetzalcoatl heard the music stop as he approached the Palace of the Sun. The musicians turned away from him, hiding their instruments. That is when Quetzalcoatl put his plan into action. Using his powers as Lord of the Winds, he summoned storm clouds dark as coal to obscure the brightness of the Sun. Then, Quetzalcoatl brought forth his own light. The musicians, terrified by the darkness of the storm clouds, saw Quetzalcoatl's light and thought it was the Sun. Relieved, they ran toward it. Quetzalcoatl gently wound his coils around the musicians and floated them down with him to Earth.

As soon as the musicians saw Smoking Mirror, they realized the Lord of the Winds had tricked them. They looked fearfully around at Earth, but they were quite surprised by what they saw. The terrible, dark place the Sun had told them about wasn't terrible at all. Earth was a colorful place, filled with exotic plants and animals. Best of all, the Sun caressed Earth with its warmth and brightness.

At the urging of Smoking Mirror and Quetzalcoatl, the musicians began travelling throughout Earth. Everywhere they went, they brought the beauty of their music with them. The birds began to greet the dawn with a thousand different songs. The brooks and streams whispered to each other. The wind whistled through the branches of the trees. And the wolves threw back their heads and howled joyfully at the beaming moon. Thanks to the Lord of the Winds, Earth would never again be without music.

Use context clues. Think about what is going on in the last part of this paragraph. What do you think the word *caressed* means?

Notice supporting details. Which details show you that music has been brought to Earth?

ANSWER STRATEGIES

Notice the setting. The setting describes the place or places where the major action of the story takes place. Which answer choice fits that description?

1 Which of the following best describe the setting of the story?

   A. Earth and the Palace of the Sun

   B. rolling hills and tall mountains

   C. winding rivers and deep oceans

   D. Earth and the sky

Think about purpose. Choose the answer that applies to the *entire* legend.

2 What is the purpose of this legend?

   A. to describe Earth before it had music

   B. to persuade Quetzalcoatl that Earth needed music

   C. to explain how Earth acquired music

   D. to inform the reader about the relationship between the Lord of the Winds and Smoking Mirror

Identify the climax. The climax is a dramatic event that affects the entire story. Which answer choice has the most dramatic effect on the story being told?

3 Which of the following best describes the climax of the legend?

   A. Quetzalcoatl agreeing to travel to the Palace of the Sun

   B. Quetzalcoatl producing a terrible storm and carrying the musicians back to Earth

   C. the Sun commanding his musicians to stop playing music

   D. Smoking mirror demanding that Quetzalcoatl bring music to Earth

4 Which of the following is the best definition of *caressed*?

A. damaged

B. scorched

C. parched

D. embraced

> **Use context clues.** The sentence in which *caressed* is used begins, "Best of all…." Which answer choice suggests a positive definition?

5 Which of the following details does NOT show that music has been brought to Earth?

A. the wolves howl

B. the birds sing

C. the musicians travel

D. the wind whistles

> **Evaluate supporting details.** All four answer choices occur in the concluding paragraph. Which one does not directly refer to making music?

6 Describe the personalities of Smoking Mirror and Quetzalcoatl and the kind of relationship they have.

> **Plan your response.** What three things does the question ask you to describe?

Sample short response for question 6:

Smoking Mirror is a god who knows what he wants and how to get it. When he wants to speak with Quetzalcoatl, he calls "mightily" to every corner of the earth. When he has got Quetzalcoatl's attention, he doesn't just ask him to look around, he "demands" it. At the same time, he shows his softer side by noting "sadly" that Earth has no music. Quetzalcoatl is also a forceful god. He "thunders" at Smoking Mirror for disturbing his sleep and lectures him about the faithfulness of the Sun's musicians. Like Smoking Mirror, however, Quetzalcoatl also has a softer side, which he shows by agreeing to try to bring music to Earth. Both of these gods express great frustration with one another, yet in the end they respect one another enough to work together toward a common goal.

> **Study the response.** This is a strong response because the writer follows the organization expressed in the question and also because the writer quotes from the legend to support his observations.

Reading Test Practice
LONG SELECTIONS

DIRECTIONS Now it's time to practice what you've learned about reading test items and choosing the best answers. Read the following selection, "Ruins in the Mist." Use the side column to make notes about the important parts of this selection: important ideas, comparisons and contrasts, difficult vocabulary, interesting details, and so on.

Ruins in the Mist

High in the Andes Mountains of Peru, at an elevation of nearly 8,000 feet, shrouded in mist and clouds, lie the remarkably well–preserved and mysterious ruins of Machu Picchu. For nearly a century, archeologists and historians have studied the ruins, attempting to discover their origin and purpose. Machu Picchu, however, has not given up its secrets easily.

Adventure in the Andes The discovery of Machu Picchu in 1911 by a historian from Yale University is an adventure story worthy of the exploits of the fictional explorer Indiana Jones. Hiram Bingham taught Latin–American history at Yale, where he served on the history faculty from 1909 until 1924. In July of 1911, Bingham led an archeological team from Yale on an expedition to Peru. The goal of the expedition was to find the site of a city called Vilcabamba, known in archeological lore as the "Lost City of the Incas." Vilcabamba was a secret fortress in the Andes Mountains which the Inca had used as a stronghold during their rebellion against the Spanish *conquistadores* during the 16th century.

Bingham's team was seeking an elusive goal—not even the Spanish had ever discovered the location of Vilcabamba. Bingham was up to the task, however. He had learned mountain–climbing skills from his father, a Pacific missionary, and he tackled the Andes with courage and determination. The Yale team visited a number of Inca sites, but it was not until July 24 that they hit pay dirt. On that day, Melchor Arteaga, a resident of the Urubamba River valley, led Bingham to the site of spectacular Inca ruins called Machu Picchu. The ruins sat between two tall peaks—Machu Picchu (Old Peak) and Huayna Picchu (New Peak)—and they were in astonishingly good shape.

In 1912, Yale University and the National Geographic Society sponsored a Bingham–led excavation of Machu Picchu. The evidence he collected during that trip and another in 1915 convinced Bingham that he had indeed found Vilcabamba. Today, Bingham's claim is disputed. Another site Bingham discovered, Espíritu Pampa, is now thought to be the true Lost City of the Incas. So what exactly had Bingham discovered at Machu Picchu?

The City in the Clouds Additional excavations and discoveries have identified Machu Picchu as one of a series of structures along the Inca foot highway that wound its way through the Andes. Some of these structures were fortified strongholds, others were inns for travelers, and still others were signal towers. Machue Picchu, however, seems to be none of these. The way the city is laid out and the types of buildings found there suggest that it may have been a ceremonial city or an extensive palace complex for an Inca ruler.

Machu Picchu is a city of about five square miles. The buildings likely were constructed during the mid-15th century and occupied for about a century. They include palaces, temples, baths, storage facilities, and nearly 150 houses. In addition, the site includes plazas, a cemetery, and stepped terraces for growing food which were irrigated by a system of aqueducts. At the southeastern end of the city is its only formal entrance, which leads to the Inca highway.

Near the Main Plaza is a remarkable feature called the Intihuatana, or Hitching Post of the Sun. This ceremonial sundial is positioned to indicate important astronomical events and suggests that one of Machu Picchu's purposes may have been as an astronomical observatory.

A City Reborn Machu Picchu is believed to have been abandoned some time after the Spanish conquest of Cuzco in 1533. By this time the supply lines between the major Inca social centers had been interrupted by the rebellion against Spain, and the Inca empire crumbled.

Today, however, Machu Picchu is bustling again—this time with tourists. The ruins are the most lucrative tourist attraction in all of Peru. Some visitors arrive by railroad and bus, a trip that can be made in a day. Other travelers prefer to hike the ancient Inca highway. Although this trip can take as long as six days, hikers get the thrill of climbing up thousands of stone-cut steps, past high retaining walls, and through tunnels, all examples of Inca engineering skill. Although its original purpose may never be discovered, Machu Picchu has been discovered by tourists from around the world. In 1983, UNESCO honored the skill and daring of Machu Picchu's founders and builders by declaring the ruins a World Heritage site.

Now answer questions 1–6. Base your answers on the selection, "Ruins in the Mist."

1 What is the author's purpose for writing about Machu Picchu?

   A. to persuade the reader that Machu Picchu is the most mysterious of Peru's ancient ruins

   B. to describe the discovery of Machu Picchu and the structures it contains

   C. to explain why Machu Picchu is Peru's most lucrative tourist attraction in Peru

   D. to inform readers about the exploits of Hiram Bingham

2 Read this sentence from the selection:

   Bingham's team was seeking an elusive goal— not even the Spanish had ever discovered the location of Vilcabamba.

   Which of the following is the best definition for *elusive*?

   A. difficult to pin down

   B. easy to understand

   C. simple to find

   D. effortless to achieve

3 Which of the following best describes Machu Picchu?

   A. fortress

   B. signal tower

   C. inn for travelers

   D. ceremonial city or palace complex

4 Which of the following is NOT found at Machu Picchu?

A. palaces

B. plazas

C. ball courts

D. temples

5 What is the main idea of the section titled "A City Reborn"?

A. Historians don't understand the purpose of Machu Picchu.

B. Machu Picchu was abandoned after the rebellion against Spain.

C. Machu Picchu has become a popular destination for tourists.

D. Machu Picchu is now a UNESCO World Heritage site.

6 Why was Hiram Bingham especially qualified to lead the Yale expedition to find the Lost City of the Incas?

THINKING IT THROUGH

The notes in the side columns will help you think through your answers. See the answer key at the bottom of the next page. How well did you do?

Remember that the author's purpose relates to the entire piece of writing, not to just one paragraph or section.

1 What is the author's purpose for writing about Machu Picchu?

A. to persuade the reader that Machu Picchu is the most mysterious of Peru's ancient ruins

B. to describe the discovery of Machu Picchu and the structures it contains

C. to explain why Machu Picchu is Peru's most lucrative tourist attraction in Peru

D. to inform readers about the exploits of Hiram Bingham

Three of the answer choices begin with words that suggest "ease," even though the sentence quoted ends by suggesting "difficult."

2 Read this sentence from the selection:

> Bingham's team was seeking an elusive goal— not even the Spanish had ever discovered the location of Vilcabamba.

Which of the following is the best definition for *elusive*?

A. difficult to pin down

B. easy to understand

C. simple to find

D. effortless to achieve

Reread the first paragraph of the section "City in the Clouds." Which answer choices does the writer dismiss as unlikely?

3 Which of the following best describes Machu Picchu?

A. fortress

B. signal tower

C. inn for travelers

D. ceremonial city or palace complex

4 Which of the following is NOT found at Machu Picchu?

   A. palaces

   B. plazas

   C. ball courts

   D. temples

> The key word in the question is *NOT*. Look for the answer choice that does not appear in the article.

5 What is the main idea of the section titled "A City Reborn"?

   A. Historians don't understand the purpose of Machu Picchu.

   B. Machu Picchu was abandoned after the rebellion against Spain.

   C. Machu Picchu has become a popular destination for tourists.

   D. Machu Picchu is now a UNESCO World Heritage site.

> The correct answer here is the one that describes the entire section, not just one or two sentences.

6 Why was Hiram Bingham especially qualified to lead the Yale expedition to find the Lost City of the Incas?

Hiram Bingham was a professor of history at Yale University. His specialty was Latin-American history, and Peru is part of Latin America. Although exploring the Andes Mountains is difficult, Bingham was an experienced mountain climber, having learned the skill from his father. Finally, the article describes Bingham as courageous and determined. All of these qualities made Bingham especially qualified to lead the expedition to Peru.

> This response received a top score because it
> - stays focussed on the question
> - includes details from the article
> - ends with a sentence that echoes the question

Answers:
1. B, 2. A, 3. D, 4. C, 5. C

Reading Test Model
SHORT SELECTIONS

DIRECTIONS The strategies you have just learned can also help you with this shorter selection about the Chilean poet Gabriela Mistral. As you read the selection, respond to the notes in the side column.

When you've finished reading, answer the multiple-choice questions. Use the side–column notes to help you understand what each question is asking and why each answer is correct.

Passionate Poet

In 1945, a Chilean educator, diplomat, and poet became the first Latin American to be awarded the Nobel Prize for Literature. Born on April 7, 1889, in the village of Vicuña in northern Chile, Lucila Godoy Alcayaga was of Spanish, Basque, and Indian descent. She grew up with a love for learning and became a schoolteacher at the age of fifteen. Eventually, she rose to the position of college professor.

In 1914, Alcayaga won a Chilean poetry prize for three sonnets titled "Sonetos de la muerte" ("Sonnets of Death). However, the sonnets did not bear the name Lucila Godoy Alcayaga. Instead, they were signed Gabriela Mistral, a mixture of the names of her two favorite poets, Gabriele D'Annunzio and Frédéric Mistral.

Poetry was not Mistral's only passion. She also served as a Chilean culture minister and diplomat, representing her country in Spain, Portugal, Italy, and France, among other countries.

READING STRATEGIES FOR ASSESSMENT

Note important details. What details expand the topic sentence in this paragraph?

A tragic romance when she was young may be partly responsible for the passion and emotional power of her poetry. The two most prominent themes in Mistral's work are her love for children and her deep feelings for the people of Latin America, especially the disadvantaged. Gabriela Mistral died in Hempstead, New York, on January 10, 1957.

See connections. Which part of Mistral's background might explain her deep feelings for the people of Latin America?

ANSWER STRATEGIES

1 Which of the following best explains the purpose of this biographical sketch?

A. to persuade the reader that Mistral is the most important writer in Latin American history.

B. to describe Mistral's love of education

C. to inform the reader about Mistral's life and work

D. to entertain the reader with stories from Mistral's life

> **Understand the writer's purpose.** Persuading and entertaining are clearly incorrect choices. Of the two remaining choices, which one covers the entire selection?

2 Which of the following was NOT one of Mistral's careers?

A. elected government official

B. diplomat

C. professor

D. poet

> **Read details carefully.** Did Mistral have a career in government service? Was she ever elected to a government post?

3 Which of the following best explains Mistral's deep feelings for the people of Latin America?

A. being born in a small village

B. her career as a diplomat

C. being of Spanish, Basque, and Indian descent

D. becoming a schoolteacher at fifteen

> **Make reasonable assumptions.** Which answer choice mentions the variety of people who live in Latin America?

Answers:
1. C, 2. A, 3. C

Read the title. What does the title tell you about the information displayed in these graphs?

_____

_____

_____

Read the key. Which pattern represents the rural population? The urban population?

_____

_____

_____

DIRECTIONS Some test questions ask you to analyze a visual rather than a reading selection. Study the two graphs below and answer the questions that follow.

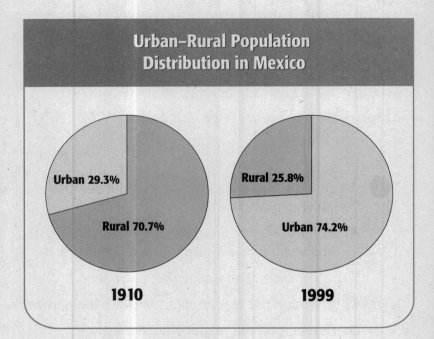

Urban–Rural Population Distribution in Mexico

Urban 29.3%

Rural 70.7%

1910

Rural 25.8%

Urban 74.2%

1999

ANSWER STRATEGIES

Interpret the question accurately. Are cities urban or rural?

Draw conclusions based on the facts. Answer choices A and B contradict the information in the graphs. Why is answer choice D not a logical conclusion?

④ What percentage of Mexicans lived in cities in 1999?

A. 29.3

B. 74.2

C. 25.8

D. 70.7

⑤ Which of the following statements best explains what happened to Mexico's population between 1910 and 1999?

A. The majority of Mexicans returned to farmlands.

B. The urban population shrank.

C. The majority of Mexicans migrated to cities.

D. Mexico produced less and less food.

Reading Test Practice
SHORT SELECTIONS

DIRECTIONS Use the following to practice your skills. Read the selection carefully. Then answer the multiple-choice questions that follow.

A Musical Legend

On July 17, 2003, a musical legend in the Latino community of the United States took her final bow. Celia Cruz died of cancer after a long musical career that took her from the nightclubs of Havana, Cuba, to the White House, where she received the National Medal of Arts from President Clinton in 1994.

After graduating from high school, Cruz studied to become a literature teacher. Her studies were put on hold when she won an amateur talent show and decided to try her luck at singing. Cruz took voice and musical theory classes at the Havana Conservatory of Music, and in 1950 she began singing with one of Cuba's most popular orchestras, *La Sonora Matancera*. She and the orchestra became fixtures on radio and television and even appeared in five movies.

In 1961, Cruz came to live in the United States. Although she made nearly thirty recordings during the 1960s, she failed to achieve the popularity she had enjoyed in Cuba—until, that is, she discovered the dance music called salsa. Cruz soon became a musical idol to a new generation of Latinos, infusing salsa with new life by adding her own distinctive style. In 1988, the British Broadcasting Company produced a documentary about her life. She appeared in the films *The Mambo Kings* and *The Perez Family* during the 1990s, when she also won a Grammy award for her recording *Ritmo en el corazón*. Cruz was also awarded an honorary doctorate in music from Yale University.

Although Celia Cruz never became the literature teacher she longed to be as a young girl, she nevertheless spent her life teaching lessons to her legions of admiring fans—lessons about determination, living life to the fullest, and believing in yourself and your dreams.

1 What is the main idea of this selection?

   A. Celia Cruz won many honors during her lifetime.

   B. Celia Cruz found fame and respect as a singer and entertainer.

   C. Celia Cruz was a star of Cuban radio and television.

   D. Celia Cruz popularized the dance music called salsa.

2 Which of the following best defines the word *infusing*?

   A. to add something

   B. defining

   C. take something away

   D. changing

DIRECTIONS Use the chart below to answer the questions that follow.

Comparing Population Growth: Mexico City and Buenos Aires					
	Population (millions)				
	1950	1970	1990	2000	2015 (projected)
Mexico City, Mexico	3.1	9.1	15.1	18.1	19.2
Buenos Aires, Argentina	5.0	8.4	10.6	12.6	14.1

Source: The New York Times Almanac, **2003**

3 What was the population of Buenos Aires in 1990?

A. 10.6

B. 15.1

C. 8.4

D. 9.1

4 When does the chart show the population of Mexico City exceeding that of Buenos Aires?

A. 2000

B. 1950

C. 1970

D. 1990

5 When does the chart show the population of Mexico City nearly doubling?

A. between 1950 and 1970

B. between 1950 and 1990

C. between 1990 and 2000

D. between 1970 and 2000

THINKING IT THROUGH

The notes in the side column will help you think through your answers. Check the key at the bottom of this page. How well did you do?

ANSWER STRATEGIES

1 What is the main idea of this selection?

Read the question carefully. It asks for the main idea of the entire selection, not just one paragraph.

A. Celia Cruz won many honors during her lifetime.

B. Celia Cruz found fame and respect as a singer and entertainer.

C. Celia Cruz was a star of Cuban radio and television.

D. Celia Cruz popularized the dance music called salsa.

2 Which of the following best defines the word *infusing*?

If you look at the context of *infusing*, you'll notice a word that appears in one of the answer choices.

A. to add something

B. defining

C. take something away

D. changing

3 What was the population of Buenos Aires in 1990?

Read down and across carefully to find the correct answer.

A. 10.6

B. 15.1

C. 8.4

D. 9.1

4 When does the chart show the population of Mexico City exceeding that of Buenos Aires?

A. 2000

B. 1950

C. 1970

D. 1990

5 When does the chart show the population of Mexico City nearly doubling?

A. between 1950 and 1970

B. between 1950 and 1990

C. between 1990 and 2000

D. between 1970 and 2000

Answers:
1. B, 2. A, 3. A, 4. C, 5. D

Functional Reading Test Model

DIRECTIONS Study the following information from the back of a bottle of Sof–Ray Sunscreen Lotion. Then answer the questions that follow.

Excessive exposure to the sun's rays can lead to premature aging of the skin, other signs of skin damage, and some forms of skin cancer. Regular use of Sof-Ray Sunscreen Lotion according to the following directions may reduce the effects of overexposure to the sun.

Sof–Ray Sunscreen Lotion is water–resistant, PABA–free, and won't clog pores.

Sof–Ray Sunscreen Lotion is a broad–spectrum sunscreen for use by adults and children 6 months of age and older.

DIRECTIONS: Apply liberally and evenly to the skin thirty minutes before exposure to the sun. Reapply sunscreen after swimming for more than 90 minutes, towel–drying, or perspiring excessively.

The minimum recommended SPF for children under 2 years of age is 4. Consult your physician before using sunscreen on children under 6 months of age.

WARNINGS: This product is for external use only. Do not swallow. If product is accidentally swallowed, seek medical help immediately or contact your local Poison Control Center for instructions. Avoid contact with eyes. Should this product get into the eyes, rinse eyes thoroughly with cold water. Stop using this product if skin becomes irritated or a rash appears. If irritation or rash persists, seek medical assistance. Do not use on children under 6 months of age except on the advice of your physician. Keep this product and all drugs out of the reach of children.

READING STRATEGIES FOR ASSESSMENT

Read the information carefully. Each section contains important information about the use of this product, including what to do if problems occur.

Consider type style. Boldfaced words indicate the type of information that follows.

Claims are typically included with the general information or the "Indications for Use." Which answer choice appears in neither place?

Read the "Warnings" carefully to discover what to do when problems occur.

Choice "C" is obviously incorrect. Which of the remaining choices appears in the "Directions?"

1 Which of the following claims is NOT made for Sof–Ray Sunscreen Lotion?

A. lasts all day

B. PABA–free

C. won't clog pores

D. water–resistant

2 What should you do if the sunscreen gets into your eyes?

A. Call your physician.

B. Rinse thoroughly with cold water.

C. Contact your Poison Control Center.

D. Stop using the product.

3 When should you reapply the sunscreen?

A. every 90 minutes

B. after towel–drying

C. after consulting your physician

D. every 30 minutes

Functional Reading Test Practice

DIRECTIONS Study the following nutritional label for blue corn tortilla chips. Circle the information that you think is the most important. Then answer the multiple–choice questions that follow.

Nutrition Facts

Serving size 1 ounce (28g)
Servings Per Container 10

Amount Per Serving

Calories 130
Calories from Fat 45

	% Daily Value*
Total Fat 5g	8%
Saturated Fat 1g	5%

Cholesterol 0mg	0%
Sodium 300mg	12%
Total Carbohydrate 20g	7%
Dietary Fiber 2g	8%
Sugars 0g	
Protein 2g	

Vitamin A 0% • Vitamin C 0%
Calcium 4% • Iron 0%

* Percent Daily Values are based on a 2,000 calorie diet.

1. How many grams of saturated fat does this package of chips have?
   - **A.** 1g
   - **B.** 5g
   - **C.** 10g
   - **D.** 50g

2. How many calories do three servings of chips have?
   - **A.** 390
   - **B.** 135
   - **C.** 1,300
   - **D.** 450

3. The total fat in one serving of chips represents what percent daily value?
   - **A.** 5%
   - **B.** 8%
   - **C.** 45%
   - **D.** 80%

4. How much does one serving of chips weigh in grams?
   - **A.** 1
   - **B.** 10
   - **C.** 20
   - **D.** 28

THINKING IT THROUGH

The notes in the side column will help you think through your answers. Check the answer key at the bottom of the page. How well did you do?

Notice that the question is about the entire package, so you'll have to multiply by the number of servings the package holds to get the correct answer.

1 How many grams of saturated fat does this package of chips have?

A. 1g

B. 5g

C. 10g

D. 50g

Again, multiplication is the key to find the correct answer.

2 How many calories do three servings of chips have?

A. 390

B. 135

C. 1,300

D. 450

Read the label carefully to locate the % Daily Value for total fat.

3 The total fat in one serving of chips represents what percent daily value?

A. 5%

B. 8%

C. 45%

D. 80%

This information is supplied along with "ounces" on the label.

4 How much does one serving of chips weigh in grams?

A. 1

B. 10

C. 20

D. 28

Revising-and-Editing Test Model

DIRECTIONS Read the following paragraph carefully. Then answer the multiple-choice questions that follow. After answering the questions, read the material in the side columns to check your answer strategies.

¹ The Maya was one of the importantest civilizations in Central America. ² As early as 1500 B.C. the Maya lived in villages and they practiced agriculture and they used advanced agricultural techniques, such as irrigation. ³ They made paper from the bark of wild fig trees and used this paper to make books filled with hieroglyphic writing. ⁴ The Maya also worked gold copper and other metals. ⁵ Long before the Spanish arrived, the Maya had calenders and advanced knowledge of astronomy.

1 Which of the following is the best way to revise the first half of sentence 1?

   A. The Maya were one of the importantest civilizations…

   B. The Maya was one of the most important civilizations…

   C. The maya was one of the most important civilizations…

   D. The Maya were one of the most important civilizations…

2 Which sentence in the paragraph is a run-on?

   A. sentence 2

   B. sentence 4

   C. sentence 1

   D. sentence 5

Watch for common errors. Highlight or underline errors such as incorrect punctuation, spelling, or punctuation; fragments or run-on sentences; and missing or misplaced information.

ANSWER STRATEGIES

Verb Agreement and Comparisons *Maya* is plural and requires a plural verb form. The superlative form of the modifier *important* is not formed by adding *–est.*

Run-on Sentences Two or more complete thoughts run together with no punctuation is a run-on sentence.

Separating Complete Thoughts
Separate the complete thoughts in a run–on sentence by dividing the sentence into two sentences. Use a period and a capital letter.

3 Which of the following is the best way to fix sentence 2?

A. …the Maya lived in villages, and they practice agriculture, and they used…

B. …the Maya lived in villages and practiced agriculture. They used…

C. …the Maya lived in villages and practiced agriculture: they used…

D. …the Maya lived in villages, they practiced agriculture. They used…

Items in a Series Items in a series should be separated by commas. If one or more items in the series already has a comma, then separate the items with semicolons.

4 What change, if any, should be made to sentence 4?

A. no change

B. gold, copper and other metals

C. gold, copper, and other metals

D. gold; copper; and other metals

Spelling Always check to be sure words are spelled correctly.

5 What change, if any, should be made in sentence 5?

A. Change *calender* to *calendar*.

B. Change *advanced* to *advance*.

C. Change *calender* to *calandar*.

D. no change

Answers:
1. D, 2. A, 3. B, 4. C, 5. A

Revising-and-Editing Test Practice

DIRECTIONS Read the following paragraph carefully. As you read, circle each error that you find and identify the error in the side column—for example, *misspelled word* or *incorrect punctuation*. When you have finished, circle the letter of the correct choice for each question that follows.

¹ The ethnic makeup of Puerto Rico is shaped by immigration to the island. ² When Columbus arrived at the island in 1493. ³ There was between 20,000 and 50,000 Taino Indians living there. ⁴ Soon, disease and mistreatment by europeans reduced the Indian population greatly. ⁵ The Spanish brang a small number of African slaves with them to the island. ⁶ During the 19th century, immigrants to the island included the following Chinese, Italians, Germans, Lebanese, Corsicans, Irish, and Scottish.

1 What change, if any, should be made to sentence 1?

   A. Change *immigration* to *emigration*.

   B. Change *is* to *was*.

   C. Change *island* to *Island*.

   D. No change is needed.

2 Sentence 2 is a fragment. Which of the following shows the best way to fix the fragment?

   A. Add it to the end of sentence 1.

   B. Add it to the beginning of sentence 3 with a semicolon after *1493*.

   C. Add it to the beginning of sentence 3 with a comma after *1493*.

   D. Add it to the end of sentence 1 with a comma after *immigration to the island*.

3 What change, if any, should be made to sentence 3?

  A. Change *was* to *were*.

  B. Change *there* to *their*.

  C. Change *between* to *about*.

  D. No change is needed.

4 Which word in sentence 4 is misspelled?

  A. disease

  B. europeans

  C. mistreatment

  D. Indian

5 What change, if any, should be made to sentence 5?

  A. Change *island* to *Island*.

  B. Change *African* to *african*.

  C. Change *brang* to *brought*.

  D. No change is needed.

6 What punctuation is missing in sentence 6?

  A. semicolon after *following*

  B. colon after *following*

  C. comma after *following*

  D. dash after *following*

THINKING IT THROUGH

Use the notes in the side columns to help you understand why some answers are correct and others are not. Check the answer key on the next page. How well did you do?

1 What change, if any, should be made to sentence 1?

   A. Change *immigration* to *emigration*.

   B. Change *is* to *was*.

   C. Change *island* to *Island*.

   D. No change is needed.

> Remember that verb tense should be consistent within a paragraph. What tense do the verbs in the rest of the paragraph take?

2 Sentence 2 is a fragment. Which of the following shows the best way to fix the fragment?

   A. Add it to the end of sentence 1.

   B. Add it to the beginning of sentence 3 with a semicolon after *1493*.

   C. Add it to the beginning of sentence 3 with a comma after *1493*.

   D. Add it to the end of sentence 1 with a comma after *immigration to the island*.

> Sentence 1 makes no sense if you read it with sentence 2 attached at the end, so two answer choices can be eliminated. Treat the fragment as an introductory clause to sentence 3.

3 What change, if any, should be made to sentence 3?

   A. Change *was* to *were*.

   B. Change *there* to *their*.

   C. Change *between* to *about*.

   D. No change is needed.

> Subjects and verbs must agree. That is, a plural subject must have a plural verb. What is the subject of sentence 3? Is it singular or plural?

Remember that proper nouns must be capitalized. Which proper noun is not capitalized in sentence 4?

4 Which word in sentence 4 is misspelled?

A. disease

B. europeans

C. mistreatment

D. Indian

Irregular verbs form the past tense is many different ways. Which answer choice has to do with a verb?

5 What change, if any, should be made to sentence 5?

A. Change *island* to *Island*.

B. Change *African* to *african*.

C. Change *brang* to *brought*.

D. No change is needed.

Colons are used to signify that a list follows.

6 What punctuation is missing in sentence 6?

A. semicolon after *following*

B. colon after *following*

C. comma after *following*

D. dash after *following*

Writing Test Model

DIRECTIONS Many tests ask you to write an essay in response to a writing prompt. A writing prompt is a brief statement that describes a writing situation. Some writing prompts ask you to explain *what, why,* or *how.* Others ask you to convince someone about something.

As you analyze the following writing prompts, read and respond to the notes in the side columns. Then look at the response to each prompt. The notes in the side columns will help you understand why each response is considered strong.

Prompt A

Because the United States is home to many cultures, it is also home to many cuisines. Think about the ethnic foods you have tasted. Which cuisine do you enjoy the most?

Now write an essay that describes your favorite cuisine. Be specific about the foods you enjoy and list the reasons why.

Strong Response

Midweek at Lincoln Prep offers a special treat. Each Wednesday, the cafeteria features the cuisine of a different culture. I've enjoyed curries from India, satays from Thailand, and felafel from Israel. Pasta from Italy is always a popular choice, as is Japanese tempura and onion soup from France. I have to confess, however, that my favorite dishes can be found south of the Rio Grande in Mexico.

I've been eating Mexican food most of my life, but it wasn't until our family spent two weeks touring Mexico last summer that I discovered how rich and varied Mexican cuisine really is. My favorite

Identify the topic. Read the entire prompt carefully. Underline the topic of the essay you will write.

Understand what's expected of you. The second paragraph of the prompt explains what you must do and offers suggestions on how to create a successful response.

ANSWER STRATEGIES

Draw the reader in with an interesting opening paragraph. The writer includes a number of examples to introduce her topic—Mexican food.

Include personal experiences when appropriate. The writer uses a family vacation as the backdrop for discussing Mexican food.

breakfast in Mexico City was chilaquiles, a casserole of corn tortillas and a tangy tomato sauce with a fried egg on top. During the afternoon, we'd stop at a taquería, a taco stand, for a snack of grilled meats and vegetables wrapped in soft flour tortillas and splashed with hot pepper sauce.

When we arrived in the city of Oaxaca in southwestern Mexico, the food took on a different character. One night for dinner we had pieces of tender chicken served in a sauce called mole. Moles come in many different styles, but my favorite is red mole. It's made with chiles, nuts, raisins, spices, and, I was surprised to find out, chopped chocolate! It not only tastes delicious but has an irresistible aroma.

The Yucatan peninsula offered more surprises. One night we had a whole red snapper that was baked and topped with chopped tomatoes and green olives. Another evening we sampled pieces of chicken that were wrapped in giant banana leaves and steamed.

Anyone whose idea of Mexican food is limited to what's served in typical American Mexican restaurants should take a trip to Mexico. As my family and I discovered, there's a lot more to Mexican food than sour cream and melted cheese.

Prompt B

Schools regularly test students to see how well they are doing in important subjects like science, math, language arts, and social studies. Teachers have to spend a lot of time preparing students for these tests. This often means that other subjects, such as drama, music, and art, are taught only occasionally or sometimes not at all. How important do you think it is for students to learn about music and art? Are these subjects as important as history and algebra?

Write an editorial for your school or community newspaper in which you talk about the importance of teaching the arts in school. Are you in favor of spending more time on these subjects, or are other classes more important? Be sure your position is clear and that you support your position with convincing reasons.

Strong Response

Two years ago, Jefferson High School dropped its classes in fine arts. The school council said that more class time was needed to prepare students for the Third–Year–Achievement Exams (TYAEs). Clearly, the TYAEs are an important measure of students' progress. However, preparing students to take tests is not our schools' primary mission. Schools must produce well–educated students, and that education must be balanced and well–rounded. The fine arts classes at Jefferson High School should be restored.

Identify the topic. The first paragraph offers some background information and introduces the topic you will write about. Restate the topic in your own words.

Know what's expected of you. The second paragraph of the prompt lets you know that you're going to write an editorial in which you take a position and provide arguments to support that position.

ANSWER STRATEGIES

Clearly state your opinion. The writer believes that classes in the arts should be restored.

Everyone agrees that science, math, language arts, and social studies are important subject areas. To achieve success in life, students must understand the principles of science and mathematics, how the past has shaped the present and will affect the future, and how to read well and express themselves clearly and effectively.

Equally important, however, is cultural knowledge. Music, for example, is a powerful force in teenagers' lives. Schools should teach students about the history of music, its many forms, and how it differs from one culture to the next. There is so much more to music than just rock and hip-hop.

The same is true for art. Very early in life, children of all cultures display a desire to express themselves artistically with finger paints and coloring books. As children grow, they should be taught about artistic expression throughout history and cultures—painting, drawing, sculpture, weaving, architecture, and so on. This can't be accomplished with just an occasional field trip to an art museum.

It is true that classroom time is limited and that teachers already have a hard time accomplishing everything that state and local school boards demand. Nevertheless, time must be found to incorporate the arts into school curriculums so that graduates will have more to show for their four years in high school than just mastery of the "Three Rs."

Writing Test Practice

DIRECTIONS Read the following writing prompt. Using the Strategies you've learned in this section, analyze the prompt, plan your response, and then write an essay explaining your position.

Prompt C

The public library system in your community has decided to install internet filters on all computers intended for public use. These filters will block Web sites that the library board decides are unsuitable for its patrons.

Think about internet filters. What is the purpose of these filters? How well do they work? What are the benefits and drawbacks of these filters? Then write a letter to the library board expressing your support for internet filters or your objection to them. State your argument clearly, point by point, and provide convincing support for each point you make.

Scoring Rubrics

DIRECTIONS Use the following checklist to see whether you have written a strong persuasive essay. You will have succeeded if you can check nearly all of the items.

The Prompt

☐ My response meets all the requirements stated in the prompt.

☐ I have stated my position clearly and supported it with details.

☐ I have addressed the audience appropriately.

☐ My essay fits the type of writing suggested in the prompt (letter to the editor, article for the school paper, and so on).

Reasons

☐ The reasons I offer really support my position.

☐ My audience will find the reasons convincing.

☐ I have stated my reasons clearly.

☐ I have given at least three reasons.

☐ I have supported my reasons with sufficient facts, examples, quotations, and other details.

☐ I have presented and responded to opposing arguments.

☐ My reasoning is sound. I have avoided faulty logic.

Order and Arrangement

☐ I have included a strong introduction.

☐ I have included a strong conclusion.

☐ The reasons are arranged in a logical order.

Word Choice

☐ The language of my essay is appropriate for my audience.

☐ I have used precise, vivid words and persuasive language.

Fluency

☐ I have used sentences of varying lengths and structures.

☐ I have connected ideas with transitions and other devices.

☐ I have used correct spelling, punctuation, and grammar.

Apuntes

Apuntes

Apuntes

Apuntes

Apuntes

Apuntes

Apuntes

Apuntes

Credits

Cover photo by Martha Granger/EDGE Productions

Acknowledgments

En Voces

Excerpt from *La casa en Mango Street* by Sandra Cisneros. Copyright © 1984 by Sandra Cisneros. Published by Vintage Español, a division of Random House, Inc. Translation copyright © 1994 by Elena Poniatowska. Reprinted by permission of Susan Bergholz Literary Services, New York. All rights reserved.

Excerpts from "Baby H.P." by Juan José Arreola, from Confabulario. Copyright © 1952 by Fondo de Cultura Económica. Reprinted by permission of Fondo de Cultura Económica.

"Ébano real" by Nicolás Guillén, from Antología Mayor. Copyright © 1972. Reprinted by permission of Editorial Letras Cubanas, Havana, Cuba.

Excerpt from *La casa de Bernarda Alba* by Federico García Lorca. Copyright © Herederos de Federico García Lorca. Reprinted by permission of Mercedes Casanovas Agencia Literaria, Barcelona.

Excerpts from "Amor mío: Brillo afuera, oscuridad en casa..." by Friné Sánchez Brandt, from Venezuela Farándula No. 1039. Copyright © Revista Ronda C.A.

Excerpt from *Bendíceme, Última* by Rudolfo Anaya. Copyright © 1992 by Rudolfo Anaya. Published by Warner Books, 1992. Reprinted by permission of Susan Bergholz Literary Services, New York.

"Canción de otoño en primavera" by Rubén Darío. Copyright © by Rubén Darío. Reprinted by permission.

Excerpt from "La muñeca menor" by Rosario Ferré. © Alianza Editorial, S.A., Madrid. Reprinted by permission.

Literatura adicional

"Borges y yo" by Jorge Luis Borges. © 1995 by María Kodama. Reprinted with the permission of The Wylie Agency, Inc.

"Arte poética" by Jorge L. Borges. © 1995 by María Kodama. Reprinted with the permission of The Wylie Agency, Inc.

"Romance sonámbulo" by Federico García Lorca. Spanish language text by Federico García Lorca (*Obras completas,* Galaxia Gutenberg 1996/1997). © Herederos de Federico García Lorca. The Spanish entity hereby identified as the author of these materials under applicable law throughout the world. All rights reserved. Enquiries should be addressed to William Peter Kosmas, at kosmas@artslaw.co.uk or at 8 Franklin Square, London W149UU, England.

"Un cuentecillo triste" by Gabriel García Márquez, from *Obra periodística, Vol. I, Textos costeños* by Gabriel García Márquez. Copyright © 1981 by Gabriel García Márquez. Reprinted by permission of Agencia Literaria Carmen Balcells, S.A.

Illustration

3 Kent A. Barton; **4** Ruben de Anda; **8** *top* Kent A. Barton; *bottom* Neverne Covington; **9** Neverne Covington; **18** *top* Kent A. Barton, *bottom* Catherine Leary; **19** Catherine Leary; **23** Kent A. Barton; **24–25** Fabricio Vanden Broeck; **29** *top* Kent A. Barton, **29–31** Enrique O. Sánchez; **41** Kent A. Barton; **42** Mike Reagan; **52** Kent A. Barton

Photography

13 Sipa Press; **14** Gary Payne/Getty Images; **35** UPI/Bettmann/Corbis; **46** UPI/Bettmann/Corbis; **47** Godo-Foto; **53** Fundación Federico García Lorca; **58** *bottom* Courtesy Venevisión; **63** Françoise de Mulder/Corbis; **65** UPI/Bettmann/Corbis; **117** Peabody Museum, Harvard University (Photo Number T3312); **119** Giuliana Traverso/Grazia Neri; **123** *clockwise from top* Yann Arthus-Bertrand/Corbis, Breck P. Kent, Jeff Scovil, Vittoriano Rastelli/Corbis, Breck P. Kent; **127** Sophie Bassouls/Corbis Sygma; **135** The Granger Collection, New York; **137** A.J. Copley/Visuals Unlimited, Inc.